WHAT LEADERS ARE SAYING...

I think every Pastor and layman should read and understand this book. The tremendous amount of pressures that a Pastor feels and experiences in the everyday administering of the call of God to his flock is beyond the average churchgoer's understanding. The things they face and the way their congregation can treat their pastors are talked about in this book, and will help you know how to cope and treat your Pastor. I personally thank you, Gary, for writing this much-needed work.

Dr. Ken Hutcherson,
Senior Pastor,
Antioch Bible Church
Former NFL Linebacker

Crushed is a cry for help from pastors across this nation. Dr. Pinion has done a masterful job by painting and portraying a picture of the plight in the pulpits of churches across America. He also expresses a passionate heart for helping pastors and wives that are seeking relief from the perils of ministry. This is a very encouraging and enlightening book and a must read for pastors, lay leaders and congregations.

Dr. John A. Gross
Director of Development
National Church Planting Office

This book should be required reading in seminary, in churches, and for pastors so that we all can take the right steps to protect and preserve pastors who are called to the brutal battle of ministry. The hope of churches lies in the pastors who lead them and the hope of pastors lies in their restoration from their crushing experiences. This book is a 'must read' for the recovery of many crushed pastors, for the correction of many parishioners who take sport in crushing pastors, and to most parishioners who have no idea of what their pastors go through.

Dr. John Morgan PhD, Lead Pastor
Pinon Hills Community Church
Farmington, NM

Dr. Gary Pinion's insight into the maze of ministry is unprecedented. His wealth of valuable information comes from the battlefield we sometimes call ministry. Gary is fresh and thought provoking, as you will also realize after reading this gold standard resource. I am happy to know and love Gary as a dear and precious friend. This is a must read for all of those endeavoring to make a difference.

Jamey Ragle
Life Building Ministries
www.reachtheplanet.org

CRUSHED
The Perilous Side of Ministry

Published by 21st Century Press
Springfield, MO 65807

21st Century Press
2131 W. Republic Rd.
PMB 41
Springfield, MO 65807

ISBN 978-0-9771964-2-5

Cover: Lee Fredrickson
Book Design: Terry White

Visit our website at: www.21stcenturypress.com

21st CENTURY
PRESS
PUBLISHING WITH PURPOSE
WWW.21STCENTURYPRESS.COM

DEDICATION

To my precious grandchildren Rakael, Savana, Madasyn, Trevor, Tharyn and Kade, who are the source of my encouragement!

TABLE OF CONTENTS

FOREWORD

Gary Pinion confronts the perils of the ministry in his riveting new book, *Crushed*. He examines the crisis of the ministry today, the devastation of dismissed pastors, and the need for their recovery. Every pastor, elder, deacon and church member needs to read this book.

Some books are meant to be read once. Some twice. This book is meant to last a lifetime. You will find yourself referring to it again and again. You will also find yourself recommending it to others. But most often, you will find yourself in its pages—looking for help, hope and comfort.

Gary Pinion examines the failures, exposes the excuses, and expresses hope for the future. His practical step-by-step suggestions are exactly what hurting pastors need today. This book is written from the heart with personal passion, powerful insight and a prophetic call to action. Don't miss it—there is nothing like it!

Dr. Ed Hindson
Assistant Chancellor
Liberty University
Lynchburg, Virginia

INTRODUCTION

Cynicism...Depression...Emotions...Burnout... Addictions...Conflicts...Budgets...Divorce...Dysfunction...Expectations...Frustration...*Ad nauseum ad infinitum!* Mix these elements with cultural environments that used to take decades or even centuries to happen, but now spring upon us in microseconds. Stir in unprecedented shifts in moral, social and economic conditions, and you have the formula for "crushed clergy," many of whom are left emotionally bruised, battered, beaten, broken and barely alive—thus unable to lead and direct the sheep in local congregations all across America.

I remember reading about one pastor speaking of what he termed, "ministerial energy depletion," who wrote sarcastically in his journal:

> If I wanted to drive a manager up the wall, I would make him responsible for the success of an organization and give him no authority. I would provide him with unclear goals, not commonly agreed upon by the organization. I would ask him to provide a service of an ill-defined nature, apply a body of knowledge having few absolutes, and staff his organization

9

with only volunteers who donate just a few hours a week at the most. I would expect him to work 10 to 12 hours per day and have his work evaluated by a committee of 300 to 500 amateurs. I would call him a minister and make him accountable to God.

Widespread evidence shows that pastoral ministry is in trouble. Greg Asimakoupoulos began a review of two books on the pastoral crisis in *Leadership* magazine with these words, "Warning: the list of endangered species is growing. To bald eagles, koalas and spotted owls, add another: ordained pastors energized by what they do." He goes on to claim that the majority of American ministers are suffering from burnout.

The two books Asimakoupoulos reviewed have ominous titles: *Pastors at Risk,* by H. B. London and Neil Wiseman, and *Pastors Off the Record,* by Stefan Ulstein. London and Wiseman quote a Focus on the Family study that claims that 70 percent of the pastors surveyed wonder if they should remain in ministry. The conclusion: "Pastors are discouraged and often outraged."

One pastor emailed Encouragement Dynamics, the ministry of which I am founder and president, saying, "I'm so mad, frustrated and outraged that I feel like shooting myself or someone."

Being a pastor today has been called the "perplexed profession." The communities in which we work no longer value our product or our role the way society once honored the church and its ministry. We are providing a service to a world that no longer wants it. We work and speak for God in a world that recognizes no God, a world in which it is not politically correct to speak openly of God.

An article in *USA Today*, dated Thursday, June 17, 2004, has the ominous title, "Clergy In Danger of Being Left Behind." The article's premise is that millions of Americans don't go to church because they can get as much information about their faith from the media (e.g., books, internet, music, television, film) as from their churches.

While getting ready to come to the office this morning, I heard on the news that a judge in a town in North Carolina is being pressured to substitute the Koran instead of the Bible for witnesses to put their right hand on and swear to tell "the truth and nothing but the truth." A Christian was then interviewed who said that America is slowly being converted to the Muslim faith.

George Hunter, the "Church Doctor," claims that America is the largest mission field in the Western world. He noted that the percentage of practicing evangelical Christians in Uganda, once a western mission field, is higher than America.

Being a pastor today is more difficult than any other time in history. This century has witnessed the collapse of the Christian consensus that has held

American culture together for centuries. The moral relativism that accompanies a secular view of reality deeply affects the work of the church and its ministry.

Contemporary pastors—the primary decision makers who provide vision and cultivate the spiritual life of the church—are caught in these frightening spiritual and social tornadoes, which are now raging throughout home, church, community and culture. The pastor's position today can be likened to the portentous clouds of a west Texas storm in July, spitting out a devastating cyclone. No one knows where the next twister might touch down or what valuables the storm will destroy.

Churches all across this nation are in disarray. Pastors are being terminated because of an emergence of a few rebellious, religious zealot "control freaks." These religious zealots are inflicting hurt on one another as well as their pastor. This disarray is also coming from a few pastors who choose to use a dictatorial style of leadership. Business meetings with yelling, fighting, threats and harsh words become the Christian version of Survivor. By lying and forming power plays and alliances against their brothers and sisters in Christ, Christians act like unbelievers. I talked to a pastor recently who told me that a former church member is suing him and his associate!

Then you have good, honest, sincere, committed, dedicated and devoted people in our churches who just want to love Jesus and love what Jesus loves, but are injured from the flying shrapnel of "spiritual grenades" thrown from inside their own ranks. These people can understand being wounded by the world, but they come to church hoping for better treatment. When they realize that the church that they thought would provide the answers to all their problems turns out to be the instigator of many of their problems, they head out the back door. Many of these innocent victims become a part of the 23 million Americans who claim Jesus as their Savior but have no discernible church connection.

Why are so many pastors and churches experiencing such devastation? Why do Christians, many of whom have been raised and trained under some of the godliest pastors and churches in America, end up acting like pagans?

This book addresses what is going on in the ministry environment of the 21st Century. The stories and ideas in the pages ahead reflect real experiences of real people in real circumstances, living out their sometimes difficult and complicated lives in what is known as the "church" world.

H. B. London and Neil B. Wiseman, in their updated edition of *Pastors at Great Risk,* say, "The risks in ministry are greater than ever. Pastors are working harder in a world that's more corrupt. They wonder why their parishioners expect them to squander energy on trivial matters when evil threatens to wreck the human race. Fatigue shows in the eyes of pastors.   Worry slows their stride. Vagueness dulls their preaching.

"This struggle takes a terrible toll, as pastors wrestle with crammed calendars, hectic homes, splintered dreams, starved intimacy and shriveled purpose. Some quit in utter hopelessness.   Others lapse into passivity and many of the rest just hold on by their fingernails."

God's mercy and grace have enabled me to survive and to tell this story.   If you really want to be able to feel the pulse beat of today's church world and ministry, I invite you to read on.

Chapter 1

REASON

Is anyone paying attention?

He who thinks that he is finished is finished. How true.
Those who think that they have arrived have lost their way.
Those who think they have reached their goal have missed it.
Those who think they are saints are demons.
—Henri Nouwen, *The Genesse Diary*

As you begin this book, let me make it very plain that I am a Barnabas. My gift is "encourager." My wiring is totally, 100 percent positive! As John Maxwell once said, "You type and cross match my blood and it is "Be Positive!" (For real). I am an extreme optimist. My ministry is Encouragement Dynamics. You may not get very far into this book before you say to yourself, "I thought this guy was a Barnabas, an encourager, an optimist, a positive man with a ministry called Encouragement

Dynamics. Well it sure doesn't sound like it to me!"
Please, I do not write this book as a doomsayer but as
an instigator of change. I have truly walked miles and
miles in the moccasins of those of whom I speak. I
have definitely "been there and done that" and experienced for myself many of the examples you will be
reading in the pages that follow.

We can learn something from everyone, but we
can learn a lot more from those who have been
through both the good times and the bad times.
Those who have taken the time to assess their experiences and are willing to share this painfully gained
wisdom with others!

Have you ever felt beaten by the world?
Have you ever felt that your spirit had been
stripped and left bare to the harsh elements?
Have you ever felt that no one cares about
your future?

I have been there. I was the one lying on the
side of the road as many passed by. They continued on—unconcerned or unaware of my
need.

But today I am thankful. Thankful for the
one who did stop and reach out. One who

took the time to bring comfort to my
wounds. One who supported me when I
could not stand on my own. One who cared
enough to see hope in my future.

I can share this story with you because of one
...one who became my "neighbor" and extended
the love of God to me.

—*The Traveler*

I do not write this book with the assumption that
I am an expert and know all there is concerning the
status of today's pastors, the state of the churches in
America in the 21st Century, or the environment that
engulfs the evangelical church as we know it today.

Nor do I boast of having a claim to fame with a
modern day spiritual pharmaceutical miracle "cure all
pill" that will fix all the problems, perplexities, pressures and pain that churches and God's chosen servant leaders are experiencing in today's world.

I do, however, write this book consumed with a
burning passion in my heart planted by the Holy
Spirit and confirmed by the Word of God. My desire
is to articulate and inform the reader through my
personal observations and experiences with regard
to the state of the church and the state of the shepherds who have a God-given call upon their life to

minister in our postmodern world.

I am very well aware that a growing number of ministers are female. Some are senior ministers, while many others fill a variety of posts in the ministerial leadership of the church. The principles in this book are not limited to any gender or denomination. Those who abuse clergy also tend to be females, so I have stayed with masculine references.

Let me say two things emphatically and dogmatically. First, I love the church! The church that Christ loved with ". . . a love marked by giving, not getting. Christ's love makes the church whole. His words evoke her beauty. Everything He does and says is designed to bring the best out of her, dressing her in dazzling white silk, radiant with holiness" (Ephesians 5:25-27 MSG).

The church has been, and continues to be, an integral and vital part of my life. On March 16, 1975, in a small church in Texas, I was first introduced to Jesus Christ as my personal Lord and Savior. I eat, breathe and sleep church. I have dedicated my life to the growth and health of the local church. The rest of my life will be devoted and dedicated to the church and the pastor/shepherd men who have yielded to the Divine call of God upon their lives to lead congregations across this nation.

Secondly, I love the ministry! For nearly thirty

years, I have been involved in ministry, and I am absolutely convinced that I could not have chosen any other profession, calling or vocation that would have made me any happier, fulfilled and rewarded.

I believe very strongly that, as one of my graduate school professors once said, "The ministry is an incredible call to an inadequate man to an impossible task for an indefinite period of time!"

Ministry and the church have been my world. But it is a world that makes me increasingly frustrated, and at times, if I'm completely honest, nauseated. Sociologist Jeffrey Hadden said, "The church is something like Noah's ark . . . if it weren't for the storm outside, you couldn't stand the smell inside."[1] The thing that saddens me is that the church should be the shelter from the storms of life. Many churches today have become a part of the storm.

Please do not misunderstand me; I love the church! I don't just like the church; I love it. But, I'm finding it increasingly difficult to feel at home in the arena I dearly love. Like Reggie McNeal so pointedly pens in his book, *The Present Future, Six Tough Questions for the Church*: The church "lacks spiritual purpose and missional vitality." He goes on to say, "I'm talking about the church world in North America. A world that has largely forsaken its missional covenant with God to be a part of Kingdom expansion. It has, instead, substituted its own charter of church as a clubhouse where religious people hang out with other people who think, dress, behave, vote, and believe like them."

One thing was embedded in my heart and soul early in my Christian life. It was driven to the core of my heart early in and throughout my Bible College and Graduate School days: the truth of Matthew 16:18b. In the passage, Jesus tells Peter, "On this rock I will build my church and the gates of Hades will not overcome it" (NIV). I wholeheartedly agree with Reggie McNeal and his imperative clarification on this matter when he says:

> Don't think for a minute that I'm even coming close to saying or inferring that the church is *dying*. The death of the church culture, as we know it, will not be the death of the church. The church Jesus founded is healthy, good and right! The church Jesus founded will survive until He returns. The imminent demise and the real question under discussion is, "Will the church, the unique culture in North America, survive another generation of its own inwardly focused gaze?" Are we currently looking at missing out on the very purpose for which God created the church—

which is to be an outward-facing force connecting with the not-yet-Christians of this
world whom Jesus so loved that He died for
them?

I believe (and believe Jesus believes) that the
church *should* be the place where the incompetent, the
unfinished, and even the unhealthy are welcome. We
must never forget that in Jesus' day, desperate people
who tried to get to Jesus were surrounded by "religious" people who ignored or rejected them.
✴ I believe the thing that attracted people to Jesus
was His fresh, authentic, original style in a world of
tired phrases, rigid rules and empty religion. He was
always in step with the times, without ever stepping
out of the Father's will!

The words of Jimmy Allen emphasized this point so
well when he said, "The first man in history to reach
out and voluntarily touch lepers didn't die of leprosy.
He died at the hands of religious leaders who wouldn't
have touched a leper on a bet."[2]

The church is trying to get *out of* what God is trying to get *into*—the world.[3] As Brian Medway, a New
Zealand evangelist, claims, "We have churches full of
people who love Jesus, but who don't love what Jesus
loves." The lack of evangelism in many churches
today confirms this. Eighty plus percent of all church

growth is transfer growth, not conversion growth. We're not birthing new sheep; we're just making it easier for the sheep to change flocks!

Part of the spiritual nurturing of followers of Jesus surely should involve helping them know how to introduce Jesus into conversations and how to pass along pertinent insights to people who are being drawn to God. Because we have made evangelism a sales activity in the North American church, we have reduced how much of it goes on. In many cases, we're not peddling Jesus—we're peddling the church, with the assumption that if people will come to the church and convert to "churchianity," they will get Jesus. Evangelism that will introduce Jesus to this culture will flow from people who are deeply in love with Jesus. It has happened before: in the Book of Acts. Their relationship with Jesus was what the early Christian community had to share with the world. They didn't have a Romans road, a New Testament, or any doctrinal treaties or "plan of salvation." They had Jesus, and people knew it. Their love for Him turned the world upside down.[4]

I remember an experience I had while pastoring. My wife and I were greeting the people coming through the doors to attend one of our worship services (as we were accustomed to and extremely passionate about). In came a couple that I could have sworn had just returned from one of those high testosterone biker rallies. He was lavished with all sorts of exotic tattoos. Because of my burden to reach the "down and outers" and to meet all new comers to our church at the "living level of their lives," I gave him a big hug and welcomed him to our church. Later, as he and his wife accepted Christ, were baptized, went through our new members class, were discipled and began to work in our children's ministry, he told me something that I will never forget. He said, "When we first came to your church, it was the sixth church that my wife and I had visited. You were the first pastor that looked at me and not my tattoos." Once again I was reminded that "in order for the church to change the world, there must be a change in the way the church sees the world."

Leonard Sweet, in his book, *Carpe Manana, Is Your Church Ready to Seize Tomorrow?* said, "Much of the religious world is archaistic rather than futuristic in tendency; it abjures innovation, mourning the moment, and caressing the status quo or the status quo ante. It has no interest in powering the future with anything but the present." As novelist E. L. Doctorow portrays so powerfully in his novel, *City of God,* organized religion has become utterly incapable of addressing the biggest moral and intellectual questions of the day. There are now companies that have more desire to change the world for good than the church does."

Peter Drucker said, "Every organization exists to serve people outside the organization; and when it exists to serve people inside the organization, it dies."

I'm concerned, as we look at the ecclesiastical Doppler radar, that the forecast doesn't look so good. Most churches are struggling with survival issues. For many, just staying in business financially or getting beyond a sense of defeat is the protocol. I'm concerned that the church is not making the impact it was created to have. I'm concerned about the growing numbers of "dropout Christians" who have been hurt and abused in churches that seem to see people as objects to be used for some grander scheme. I'm concerned about our high rate of pastoral burnout and the numbers of pastors being dismissed because they don't fit the corporate model now in vogue.

Thom S. Rainer, president of Church Central Associates, publisher of *ChurchCentral.com,* and dean of the Billy Graham School of Missions, Evangelism and Church Growth at the Southern Baptist Theological Seminary in Louisville, Kentucky, predicts the closing of 50,000 churches by 2010. He says, "Thousands of churches are on the precipice of closing. The conventional wisdom was that churches were tenaciously stubborn and could keep going for years. But those churches were led by the builder generation, those born before 1946. The church-going builders attended churches out of loyalty and tradition. They would often remain loyal to a church despite deteriorating quality and attendance. But boomers, busters/Gen Xers, and bridgers—born between 1977 and 1994—have no such loyalties. They see no need to remain with a church that exists out of tradition and with little care for the quality of the ministries. Though I am not happy to report this trend, the fading of the builder generation indicates the death of one out of eight churches in America today."[5]

In the United States, we do things so big that we give ourselves the illusion of success. My dearest friend and mentor, Charlie Harbin, who took me by his side just months after my conversion, recently told me, "The church today has confused church activity and church busyness and equates it to spirituality." We both agreed that church activity is a poor substitute for genuine spiritual vitality! This is a principle that will be hard for many of us to learn, but we must!

The Sunday before I was to leave to write this book was the first Sunday for Pastor Joel Osteen and his remarkable Lakewood Church in Houston, Texas, to meet in their new facility: the Compaq Center, the place the Houston Rockets once called home. They had over 30,000 people! I am by no means knocking this pastor or this great church, but if we were to look just at the success of Lakewood church, we would

come away thinking that, "all is well on planet church!"
But all statistics show that North America is the only
continent where the church is *not* growing; it's not even
keeping pace with the population growth. America is
the second highest missionary-receiving nation in the
world. On a per capita basis, Ireland sends out more
missionaries per year than we do.[6]

The most recent "hot button" seems to be, "We
need to plant more churches!" God is certainly for
planting churches and so am I. But let's not forget to
take care of the churches we have. It does us little
good in our efforts to reach our world if we are on a
record pace of seeing four thousand new churches
begin each year, when, in that same year, over seven
thousand churches close their doors and go out of
business.[7] You need not be a mathematician to realize that the result is that we have fewer churches for
more people.

Not only is church growth failing to keep up
with the nation's birthrate, but the behavior of those
who identify themselves as Christians cannot be dis-
tinguished statistically from those who make no
such claim, as we will later see. No matter how you
look at the statistics, they seem to point to the same
conclusion: The North American church exerts precious little influence on society. Pollster and author,
George Barna, has written several books detailing

the challenges faced by the modern church. In one of his works he warned, "Despite the activity and chutzpah emanating from thousands of congregations, the Church in America is losing influence and adherents faster that any other major institution in the nation." Then he predicted one of two outcomes for our nation within the next few years: either "massive spiritual revival" or "total moral anarchy."[8]

Before I go any further, I would like to make another emphatic and dogmatic statement: Not all the blame for the current illness of the church can be blamed on the sheep. There are plenty of shepherds in churches today who are disturbed by various pathological conditions within themselves and have serious personality, moral and ethical issues that tend to disrupt the lives of their families and churches.

Just this morning, as I was continuing to work on this manuscript, my cell phone rang. It was a pastor from a church I had previously consulted with two years ago. The situation he shared with me was that the former pastor of the church was back in the area and planning to start a church. Well, the reason the former pastor had to resign the church in the first place was because his wife had left him for another man (in the church). While their divorce was proceeding, the former pastor began to date a lady (in the church) who was also awaiting her divorce. All the divorces are now final, so the former pastor and his new wife are now down the road planting a new church. The former pastor, now starting the new church, e-mailed his former church members to invite any who would like to attend his new work. The hits just keep on coming!

In fact, there have been several times that I have had to recommend that a pastor resign. When it is obvious that a pastor who is to be "above reproach" lacks character, finds it difficult to fulfill the mundane tasks of a pastor, uses inappropriate humor in his messages, is careless about paying his bills, does not return phone calls, is overtly undisciplined, etc., he is a disgrace to the "sacred call" and should *not* be in the ministry!

Case in point is the increasing amount of pastors committing adultery. I remember, while pastoring in Farmington, New Mexico, in the mid 90s, receiving a free copy of the book, *If Ministers Fall, Can They Be Restored?* in the mail from Tim LaHaye. In the book was a letter from Dr. LaHaye with these words, "The Lord really burdened me to write this book after seven of my personal friends, pastors of churches of over 3,000, had destroyed their ministries during a twelve month period. One, with whom I worked as a part-time associate, was pastoring the fastest growing church in America (10,000 members in only 11 years).

During the year it took to write the book, five more minister friends fell, and during the six months it took Zondervan to publish it, three more with national ministries were destroyed."

This was before we ever had (and for many of us ever heard of) the Internet. Like nothing else in our lifetime, the Internet has forever changed the way we communicate, learn and work. The benefits of this tool are obvious in the church, where it has become a driving force in all facets of work.

Thanks to the Internet, pastors now have instant access to quality content to assist them in developing powerful sermons. In fact, shelves and shelves and endless boxes of books that could fill the largest U-Haul truck in the world can now be put on a couple of CDs. All those hoards of commentaries I used to have, that would make me (and you) look much smarter then we actually are, have since been given to an innocent seminary student. I now have them on CDs or can access them via the World Wide Web.

Missionaries serving in countries half a world away can provide timely updates to their sponsor churches with the simple click of a mouse. I have nearly eliminated altogether sending out hard copies of letters and newsletters. I now have an Encouragement eNewsletter that I shoot out monthly to all my supporters and prayer partners. Even tithing has become an online exercise, as the Internet provides church members with a convenient way to give.

Indeed, the ubiquitous nature of the Internet is having an incredibly positive impact on the efforts of the church. Ironically, this very ubiquity that allows for these positive gains can also serve to bring down even the most powerful of ministries. When used in anonymity and without accountability, the Internet can cause pastors and church staffers to fall prey to some of the vilest and abhorrent content ever created.

In times past, if a pastor or church member wanted to get involved in pornography, they would have to go to the back streets. Now, the purveyors of pornography will come right into your study and find *you*. Just an inquiry on the Google search engine can produce links to hard-core sex sites along *with* Bible study courses. And, thanks to e-mail spam, you don't even have to be surfing the Internet to find easy access to online pornography. One click access to porn web sites is now being delivered unsolicited directly into your *e*-mail inbox.

An article in *The Church Report* (www.thechurchreport.com December 2004), revealed some startling facts. Their report says, "The Internet is truly a world without boundaries. According to a leading Internet-filtering technology provider, the number of pornographic or sexually explicit web pages grew from 14 million in 1998 to 260 million in 2004. Numerous spam filtering companies have indicated that as many as 2.5 billion of the 12.4 billion spam e-mails being sent every day are pornographic in nature."

Before looking at how obscene web content is affecting the church and its leadership, it helps to better understand how pastors are currently using the Internet. In a recent survey of pastors, 89 percent reported having Internet access and had been online for an average of 3.4 years. The survey focused on the impact of online pornography in their lives. An astounding 37 percent of pastors in this survey indicated that viewing Internet pornography is an area where they presently struggle. More than one-third of all pastors indicated that they had visited a pornographic site in the past year. While these numbers may seem shocking to non-pastors, the pastors themselves did not indicate surprise.

Indeed, pastors are human and can be just as vulnerable as the rest of us, if not more so. As the shepherd of a church, the pastor often leads an isolated life. This was validated in a survey of pastors conducted by the Fuller Institute, which indicated that 70 percent of pastors said they do not have a close friend and are hesitant to develop close relationships with church members because they didn't want to appear to show favoritism. My personal experience is that 80-90 percent of pastors do not have a friend, confidant or mentor with whom they can be transparent.

When you combine this isolation with the pressures of serving a diverse congregation, it is easy to understand how some can become vulnerable to this temptation—especially those who have seen their own personal walk with God become less consistent as they attend to the needs of others.

Moral impurity is a plague that strikes pastors, leaving them unfit for spiritual leadership. In a recent *Leadership* magazine poll of pastors, 18 percent of pastors completing the survey admitted to sexual immorality or immoral acts. Of these pastors, 12 percent admitted to adultery (only 4 percent were discovered by the congregation). Six percent more had engaged in other immorality.[9]

That means possibly one pastor in every five has a major moral problem!

Chuck Colson's book, *The Body*, noted:

•   Pastors have the largest divorce rate among any other vocation.

•   One in 10 pastors have had affairs with members of their congregation.

- Twenty-five percent of pastors have been engaged in illicit affairs.

- The rise of the Internet has led countless pastors down the road of addiction to pornography.

I have had the unfortunate, heartbreaking experience of losing *my* hero, *my* pastor, *my* mentor, *my* friend, the person who led me to Christ, to the nauseous cancer and crippler of immorality.

As I crisscross this nation, speaking in churches and ministering to pastors, I'm continually shocked and amazed when I hear the atrocities pastors perpetrate on their families, friends and churches.

I hope I have articulated appropriately that I do understand both sides of the coin. But the premise of this book is to help you understand the "environment of ministry" that exists in our world today, so that we may bring health back into the life of the church.

There are three specific groups that I will attempt to target and challenge during the remaining pages of this book. The first group is God's chosen servant leaders: Pastor/Shepherds. These men are in the trenches and on the front lines of battle, attempting to change the world through the church, in the emerging post-Christian, pre-Christian, postmodern culture in which we live. This emerging postmodern culture embraces a contemporary philosophical view: they believe that there are no absolutes, there are no objective truths, there are no inherent meanings, and all of life is a matter of perspective. While the battle between a "Christian world-view" and a "secular world-view" rages, these mighty clergy warriors fight another battle in trying to get believers to live a "Christian world-life!"

My second target group is lay people in the church: People who love God, their ministers and the church, but urgently need to be educated on the "environment of ministry" in this emerging world.

But, more importantly, I want to speak to lay congregational *leaders*: Men and women who are sincere, honest, God-fearing and God-loving people, yet have gone astray and innocently nullified ". . . the Word of God for the sake of their tradition" (Matthew 15:6 NIV), and become "Clergy Killers."

The following e-mail from a stressed-out pastor exemplifies what results when this epidemic "control" issue happens in the Body of Christ:

> I sure would covet your prayers in the ongo-
> ing saga that is transpiring here. There have
> been more issues of trust that have been
> betrayed... I can't believe it and then again it

doesn't surprise me. For the life of me, I cannot understand why some information that had been given in confidence to two of my men has now been disseminated through a good measure of the church body. It is getting more and more difficult here and I'm scheduling another serious meeting next week in which I will have the deacons and the trustees present. It breaks my heart that after almost 11 years here I've been relegated by the 'core' group to a place that I'm belittled, gossiped about, and my character has been seriously maligned. When I came here almost 11 years ago, we had 13 people and that was it! I was paid 125 dollars a week and lived in a Sunday school classroom for the first three months. We had four missionaries that we supported and I worked about 90 hours a week between the church and two part-time jobs. Now we have close to 120 on Sunday mornings, 15 missionaries we support and about $50,000 dollars in our accounts. A man drives by my house to see when I'm here; he drives by the church to see when I'm there. What I give in tithes and missions has become public knowledge to the entire church body. I am not afraid of accountability, in fact I welcome it. What I do not welcome is the fact that there is a group of rebellious gossipers who are totally concerned about nothing in the church except how much money can be laid aside in a bank account.

Several years ago I was at a cross roads in my life and my ministry. God had positioned me at the place of one of those "defining moments" that occur in one's life. It was at this juncture in life that I had to make a major decision. I could relatively coast as a pastor for the remaining years of my life and ministry. I could reach, impact, and be a "change agent" in perhaps hundreds, maybe even thousands of people's lives. Or I could leave the pastorate and all the security it would provide for my wife and me and become an "agent of change," bringing encouragement and affirmation to hundreds of pastors and congregations across the nation. Thus, we could see thousands, maybe hundreds of thousands of lives changed for the Kingdom of God.

After much counsel, time alone with the Lord, praying, fasting and reading His Word, I decided to form Encouragement Dynamics, a 501c3 nonprofit ministry. Encouragement Dynamics is a ministry of encouragement, restoration, motivation and education that focuses on the needs of pastors in the 21st century. So my life calling is to be used of God by the church in North America and to serve the pastors of those churches. I am called to serve those who are desperate to embrace the entrepreneurial spirit, who have not adequately thought through their outward direction, who desire to find paradigm adjustments, and who are willing to die to our conveniences, our traditions and our preferences in order to rediscover the mission of the church and to see beyond our church walls.

Chapter 2

REALITY

It hurts so much!

I stake the future on the few humble and hearty lovers who seek God passionately in the marvelous, messy world of redeemed and related realities that lie in front of our noses.
—William McNamara

Persecution of church leaders, in the North American context, does not come from outside the church. It comes from inside the church. I have never had a pastor say to me, "I am quitting. The pagans are getting to me!" I have had more than I care to remember say, "I can't take the Christians in the church anymore. I've had it with ministry!" Fifty percent of pastors are so discouraged that they would leave the ministry if they could, but have no other way of making a living.[1]

"The Devil made me do it" is a cliché made popular by Flip Wilson years ago. I'm not personally convinced

we can blame or give credit the devil for everything
that's going on in the church today. But the picture
isn't complete without at least a dishonorable men-
tion given to the demonic stirrings in the lives of
many congregations.

Charles Haddon Spurgeon once commented,
"Satan is always doing his utmost to stay the work of
God. He hindered the Jews from building the Temple;
and today he endeavors to hinder the people of God
from spreading the Gospel. A spiritual temple is to be
built for the Most High, and if by any means the Evil
One can delay its uprising, he will stop at nothing. If
he can take us away from working with faith and
courage for the glory of God, he will be sure to do it.
He is very cunning and knows how to change his
argument and yet keep his design. He cares little how
he works, so long as he can hurt the cause of God."

Satan knows, like bowling, that if he can knock
down the "head pin," he has a much better chance of
getting the other pins to fall. He knows that if he can
get the pastors of America to stumble and fall, he will
have a better chance of getting the people in the congregation to fall.

One of Satan's primary goals is to hurt the cause
of God in whatever way he can. The Evil One has
many weapons in his arsenal that he will use, as
appropriate, with a view to achieving his aim.

Sometimes he uses opposition. Sometimes he stirs up division within the ranks of the people of God, knowing that a divided people will not work as effectively as a united people. At other times he uses the tactics of compromise, at other times the tactics of diversion, and at other times the tactics of temptation. Of *all* the weapons Satan has at his disposal, one of his most effective, which he has used time and time again to hinder the work of God, is that of discouragement.

The Devil, according to legend, once advertised his tools for sale at public auction. When the prospective buyers assembled, there was one oddly shaped tool, which was labeled "not for sale." Asked to explain why this was, the devil answered, "I can spare my other tools, but I cannot spare this one. It is the most useful implement that I have. It is called 'discouragement' and with it I can work my way into hearts otherwise inaccessible. When I get this tool into a man's heart, the way is open to plant anything there I may desire."

He knows that if he can get the people of God to become disheartened, to become discouraged, to despair over their efforts, he is well on the way to achieving his evil designs.

Spiritual leaders wrestle not against flesh and blood, but "against principalities, against powers, against the rulers of the darkness of this world, against spiritual wickedness in high places" (Ephesians 6:12).

Most of the messy muck that is tossed in mud slinging has its origins in the primordial goop of the cesspool of Satan. Innuendo, lies and elaborate scenarios of wrongdoing are constantly concocted and thrown on the walls through uncontrolled tongues spewing gossip. The Evil One has ruined more lives of honest and faithful leaders by masquerading as an Angel of Light, and getting people to believe lies as truth, than by any other means in Christian history. Rumor, not truth, is the enemy. The Father of Lies is well aware of the power of his choicest weapon. It is the dagger plunged deep that assassinates the soul of God's messengers—too often thrust by the closest confidants in unsuspecting moments.

This soul death is the work of evil spirits. It has caused many a pastor to hobble away from his service, unable to rekindle the passionate fire of God's calling again. The flame of service is snuffed out by the mocking deceit and condemning innuendos of Satan's hordes, which then gleefully turn their attention to the next in line to be devoured.

Life in the fishbowl for a pastor and his family is reality. It is not an easy assignment. Satan's mission is to hinder and undermine those who have been called by God to represent Him as shepherds. A pastor can survive life in the fishbowl, but not without the tender love, prayer, affirmation and encouragement of those he leads.

When we look into the pastoral aquarium these days, we see more and more pastors floating slowly to the top like dead goldfish. Many pastors today are burned out, worn out, frustrated and fatigued. They are weary, bruised, battered and beaten.

If ever there was a time when pastors needed encouragement and affirmation, it is now. As Aaron and Hur held up Moses' arms when he grew weary, every pastor needs the stabilizing forces of family and the laypeople in the church family to stand beside him in understanding and camaraderie.

A friend of mine, who has blazed trails in care giving to help many pastors, pastor's wives and missionaries and their wives, is psychiatrist Dr. Louis McBurney. He reports that low self-esteem is the number one problem pastors face. Why? We are in a high-demand, low-stroke profession in a culture that does not value our product or our work. We labor among people with unrealistic expectations, and deep inside we expect far more from ourselves, and from the church. It's no wonder Dr. McBurney's study identified depression as the second most identified pastoral problem.

In the September/October 2000 edition of *Physician Magazine*, Dr. Walt Larimore, vice president of medical outreach at Focus on the Family, and Rev. Bill Peel reported that, "Surveys indicate that 80 percent of pastors and 84 percent of their spouses are discouraged or are dealing with depression. (You can find this article at www.family.org, keyword search: pastor depression.) And more than 40 percent of pastors and 47 percent of their spouses report that they are suffering from burnout." In my experience and personal research on this topic, I have found these statistics corroborated across the board, and nearly every major denomination is initiating efforts to stay the tide of this church-wide epidemic.

Most pastors don't recognize or understand the signs of depression. They may realize that they are burning out, but they do not perceive the fine line between burnout and depression.

I have a dear friend who, along with his wife, experienced a major incident in the church he was pastoring. One of the staff persons, in whom the pastor had totally confided and trusted (in fact this staff member was being groomed by the current pastor to take the church upon his retirement), started vicious lies and innuendos about the pastor. This young man even accused him of stealing and embezzling money from the church. He then, after convincing about 400 members of the church of the untruths, went down the road and started another church. The pastor and his wife were, unknown to them at the time, thrust into a state of deep depression.

I remember him telling me, "For weeks I stayed in my room in my house, crawled into bed in a fetal position, pulled the covers up over my head and the only time I looked out was to check the clock to see if it was time for another pill." His wife struggled with depression and wouldn't leave the house for nearly two years.

Another pastor wrote the ministry saying:

Dr. Pinion:

When I think of you I think, "Well done thy good and faithful servant." You and your wife have been a wonderful inspiration to us when we needed encouragement the most.

I have been pastoring for 10 years and have never experienced a crisis like I experienced this year.

I had a mental breakdown, because of stress, burnout, sin and ignorance of God's direction in my life. There is a 'thing' called pride that really became a stumbling block for me. Others may not have detected it, but I finally realized it. Like Isaiah says in the sixth chapter, "I am a man of unclean lips." Satan was getting the best of me and I didn't realize it.

I went down on my knees on the sixteenth of February 2003. A few days later (after my wife contacted Encouragement Dynamics Ministry), you called me from California. I didn't know you, but the Lord did; and He, through His power, connected us.

You called me several times from all over the U.S. and checked on me regularly. You gave me Scripture when I couldn't hear it any more. You didn't tell me what I wanted to hear; you told me what God wanted me to hear.

My wife and I were encouraged so much by you!! God has given you a wonderful gift that is needed for pastors today.

If the Lord hadn't used my wife, you and your wife, GG, and the counselors you recommended, I probably wouldn't be alive today. I was so depressed that I thought the only way out was suicide! When you are in that deep, dark pit of discouragement and depression, suicide seems the only way out.

Today I am back in the pulpit, working for the Lord. And because of the Lord's leading, and the ministry of Encouragement

Dynamics, every day looks brighter and brighter. I want to deeply express my thanks and gratitude and praise to God for using you, my brother—for being there when I needed help the most.

The church thanks you for coming and leading us in a seminar on what pastors face and what happens in ministry. If we had more people like you, churches wouldn't shoot their pastors when they get wounded. They would learn to help them in every way.

I love you, Dr. P., and thank the Lord that you were there! And I thank the Lord you are still there when I need you!

This pastor literally had a gun pointed at his head ready to end his life. Wow! What a tremendous trophy of God's amazing grace!

The stealthy nature of depression among pastors makes it difficult to identify and treat. Often pastors are depressed before they even realize it or are able to admit it, unaware that the shadows of depression are haunting their lives and dismantling their ministry one day at a time.

Even more difficult is the fact that once a pastor does identify his depression, many churches are not safe places in which they may find support and healing.

Depression among pastors or their wives is still a dirty little secret that many churches do not wish to disclose, address, or help to cure. Some have said that this combination of late detection and church denial is a lethal cocktail that will be the single greatest cause of pastoral shortage and failure in the next decade. But that is only if pastors and churches do not begin to heal depression through greater understanding and a radically different view of the church and the pastorate.

In laymen's terms, the way I understand depression is that it is a sickness of an organ—the brain—and needs to be treated. It should be no different than a sickness of the heart, stomach, kidneys or any other vital organ. I believe that the church can curtail this epidemic, and insist that it must if we are to have any hope of healthy pastoral leadership in the future.

Long hours of work, coupled with unending demands, leave open the doors of discontent. It is one of the lowest paid professions, requiring considerable education and the expected ability to do most everything you can imagine in a thankless world. As one survey showed, pastors are "the most occupationally frustrated people in America," with 80 percent having low self-esteem and no close friends. Is it any wonder that many walk down the wrong avenues to feel appreciated and loved? They are overworked and underpaid; they serve with little respect in society, are vulnerable to the unlovely, and are a constant target of evil. Many ministers break under such burdens. Anyone could!

In my opinion, discouragement, the unstable, precocious and volatile environment in which pastors minister, along with the battle against the Evil One, is a sure prescription for defeat. One thing on which those who study the trends, data, statistics, etc., surrounding the church and ministry in today's world agree is: Today's pastors minister in a multifaceted world full of hurts, toxic relationships, crippled principles and mutilated morality.

The problems of today's generation are far more complex than those of previous periods of history. Things people only dabbled with in past generations have become pandemic today. There are more singles in our churches than in previous times...more divorcés and divorcées...more single parents...more who have been abused...more alcoholics...more who are addicted to drugs and pornography. We live longer; we travel more; we have smaller wars instead of bigger wars; we have many more college graduates; we work more and sleep less; we owe a lot more money; we have more women working outside the home than ever before, and a host of other disorders. Along with all of this, consider the plethora of social and cultural ills. We have more dysfunction in relationships. Consider

data that suggests that 80 percent of pastors themselves come from dysfunctional families, and you
have a powder keg ready to explode. Add to this the
microwave mentality and the consumer-oriented and
service-oriented mindset of our society. Is it any wonder that it is getting more and more difficult for pastors to even please the people who attend their
churches today, let alone deal with the social and cultural ills of the society in which they minister? We no
longer live in a world that asks, "What can I do to
help?" Rather it asks, "What will this job (or this
church) do for me?" People come to our churches
asking, "Do I like this pastor? Do I like this choir and
their music? Do I like this youth program? Do I like
these people?" And, most of all, "Will this church
meet *my* needs?"

This myopic "me-ism" has flooded our churches,
causing expectation levels to rise while commitment
levels have plummeted. Pastors are being especially
hard hit as they minister to the affluent, who, in their
consumer mentality, have higher expectations of
being served.

We have embraced the conveniences of the assembly
line, the efficient and the standardized, and have
grown in disdain for the chaotic, the unpredictable
and the disorganized. We've been all too willing to
give up having it our own way just to get it faster,

quicker and easier. And so the planet is marked by golden arches, symbols of our willingness to relinquish uniqueness and line up for more of the same. It's not that we don't like diversity, options and choices, because we clearly do. We want our color options, size options and style options. We just want them in a way that brings us greater convenience and doesn't complicate our lives. We want everything tailored to our specific tastes, while at the same time we want it available without any effort on our part.[2]

This, my friends, is the environment of ministry in the 21st century. It's this environment that adds to the difficulty of pastoring in today's world. With this in mind, it shouldn't shock us when we hear horror stories of pastors abandoning their divine call and forfeiting their families, ministries and years of servanthood because of the poison of discouragement.

We shouldn't be surprised to hear about congregations that are fussing, fighting and feuding, even to the point that they implode and shut their doors, putting "For Sale" signs out in front of their property.

I would have never dreamed our society would be debating whether the institution of marriage should be inclusive of anyone other than a man and a woman. Never in my wildest imagination did I think that I would see the day that we would be arguing over whether the Ten Commandments should or shouldn't be displayed in the courthouses of America. For the most part, it does seem that our society has experienced the "Death of Common Sense."

Today we mourn the passing of an old friend by the name of Common Sense:

Common Sense lived a long life, but died in the United States from heart failure early in the new millennium. No one really knows how old he was, since his birth records were long ago lost in bureaucratic red tape. He selflessly devoted his life to service in schools, hospitals, homes and factories, helping folks get jobs done without fanfare and foolishness. For decades, petty rules, silly laws and frivolous lawsuits held no power over Common Sense.

He was credited with cultivating such valued lessons as to know when to come in out of the rain, why the early bird gets the worm, and that life isn't always fair. Common Sense lived by simple, sound financial policies (don't spend more than you earn), reliable parenting strategies (the adults are in charge, not the kids), and it's okay to come in second. A veteran of the Industrial Revolution, the Great

Depression and the Technological Revolution, Common Sense survived cultural and educational trends, including body piercing and "new math."

But his health declined when he became infected with the "If-it-only-helps-one-person-it's-worth-it" virus. In recent decades, his waning strength proved no match for the ravages of well-intentioned but overbearing regulations. He watched in pain as good people became ruled by self-seeking lawyers.

His health rapidly deteriorated when schools endlessly implemented zero-tolerance policies. Reports of a six-year-old boy charged with sexual harassment for kissing a classmate, a teen suspended for taking a swig of mouthwash after lunch, and a teacher fired for reprimanding an unruly student only worsened his condition. It declined even further when schools had to get parental consent to administer aspirin to a student, but could not inform the parent when a female student was pregnant or wanted an abortion.

Finally, Common Sense lost his will to live as

the Ten Commandments became contraband, churches became businesses, criminals received better treatment than victims, and federal judges stuck their noses in everything from the Boy Scouts to professional sports.

Finally, when a woman, too stupid to realize that a steaming cup of coffee was hot, was awarded a huge settlement, Common Sense threw in the towel. As the end neared, Common Sense drifted in and out of logic but was kept informed of developments regarding questionable regulations such as those for low flow toilets, rocking chairs and stepladders.

Common Sense was preceded in death by his parents, Truth and Trust; his wife, Discretion; his daughter, Responsibility; and his son, Reason. He is survived by two stepbrothers: My Rights and Ima Whiner. Not many attended his funeral because so few realized he was gone.

—Author Unknown

Now add the vast array of parishioners. While the majority of believers are honest and loving, there is a growing company in the discontent category. A modern contingent of lastday human beings is placing new stresses on godly leaders. Pastors today minister to people who are genuinely heathen. They whine, complain, distance themselves, blame and use sarcasm—like little children when they don't get their way. In my twenty-plus years as a senior pastor of three churches, I have only had to terminate one staff person. It was a secretary who felt she had the "gift of gossip." After addressing her concerning this issue several times to no avail, I had to relieve her of her duties. She stormed out of my office yelling, "I'll see you in court."

This kind of behavior is often found in people who were raised in dysfunctional environments, were badly abused and never healed. These people get highly defensive at criticism or differences of opinions. They expect to be taken care of and often treat people as objects to meet *their* needs. Without God's healing hand, certain ones become victims who seek revenge on the leaders of society. Pastors are sitting ducks!

And don't leave out our own homegrown hypocrites, many who have truly risen to the level of Pharisee. These individuals devour positions of power without perceiving the need to live the life of Christ on a daily basis. Blanketing their own sins in a religious spirit, they are quick to judge and are skilled at group manipulation. Hard to move, hard to change, they hinder the progress of the tender shoots who would love to follow God. Whatever the cause of their internal pain and their uncontrolled anger, there lurks just below the surface a violent willingness to bring down those in authority.

Before I continue, let me say that I am *not*, nor do I claim to be, a sociologist, statistician or expert on statistics. I heard someone once say that, "Statistics are a lot like bathing suits. They reveal what needs to be revealed and conceal what needs to be concealed." I have, however, tried my very best to research the most recent and most credible data available. I understand and will yield to the fact (and will comment more on this later in the chapter) that the numbers concerning the world of the church can be skewed and could quite possibly go either *up* or *down*. One could argue that they (the data and statistics) are too *high* or they are to *low*. For argument's sake, let's say they *are low*! My premise would then be that they are still *high* enough for us to be deeply concerned.

Alan C. & Cheryl D. Klass, in their book, *Quiet Conversations, Concrete Help for Weary Ministry Leaders*, say, "About 100,000 parish pastors (and their families) are experiencing career burnout. Some recognize they are in trouble. Most need a way forward in ministry before they are pushed out."

The following statistics should literally break the heart of every pastor, lay leader and church member:

- Eighteen hundred pastors leave the ministry each month due to moral failure, spiritual burnout or contention in their churches.

- Four thousand new churches begin each year, but over seven thousand churches close.

- Fifty percent of pastors' marriages will end in divorce.

- Eighty percent of pastors and eighty-four percent of their spouses feel unqualified and discouraged in their role as pastors.

- Fifty percent of pastors are so discouraged that they would leave the ministry if they could, but have no other way of making a living.

- Eighty percent of seminary and Bible school graduates who enter the ministry will leave the ministry within the first five years. Ninety percent of pastors said their seminary or Bible school training did only a fair to poor job preparing them for ministry.

- Eighty-five percent of pastors said their greatest problem is they are sick and tired of dealing with problem people, such as disgruntled elders, deacons, worship leaders, worship teams, board members and associate pastors. Ninety percent said the hardest thing about ministry is dealing with uncooperative people.

- Seventy percent of pastors feel grossly underpaid.

- Ninety percent said the ministry was completely different than what they thought it would be before they entered the ministry.

- Seventy percent felt God called them to pastoral ministry before their ministry began but, after three years of ministry, only fifty percent still felt called.

Pastors' Wives:
- Eighty percent of pastors' spouses feel their spouse is overworked.

- Eighty percent of pastors' wives feel left out and unappreciated by the church members.

- Eighty percent of pastors' spouses wish their spouse would choose another profession.

- Eighty percent of pastors' wives feel pressured to do things and be something in the church that they really are not.

- The majority of pastors' wives surveyed said that the most destructive event that has occurred in their marriage and family was the day they entered the ministry.

Pastors' Marriages:
- Seventy percent of pastors constantly fight depression.

- Almost forty percent polled said they have had an extra-marital affair since beginning their ministry.

Pastors' Children:
- Eighty percent of adult children of pastors surveyed have had to seek professional help for depression.

Pastors' Relationship with the Lord:
- Seventy percent of pastors do not have a close friend, confidant or mentor.

- Ninety-five percent of pastors do not regularly pray with their spouses.

- Eighty percent of pastors surveyed spend less than fifteen minutes a day in prayer.

- Seventy percent said the only time they spend studying the Word is when they are preparing their sermons.[1]

In my effort to paint a picture of the *reality* of the ministry environment, it would certainly not be complete if I were to neglect the truth that the church (to use a good old southern term) *ain't cuttin' it* in terms of missional effectiveness.

The collapse of the church culture can be demonstrated in several ways. One is through demographics. The percentage of Americans who claim to go to church each week has run in the 40 to 43 percent range for thirty years. George Barna has even been quoted to believe that between 40 percent and 50 percent of Americans do, in a given week, go to church.[2] But can we really believe those numbers?

In my travels, I have yet to be *in* a church or to be *with* a pastor who lives in a community where 40 percent of the population shows up at church on Sunday. I asked several hundred pastors if there would even be enough seats in the church buildings in their towns to accommodate 40 percent of their town's population if they were to come to church on any given Sunday. They overwhelmingly said, "No!"

Think about it! I'm not even sure if many towns I know of would have room for 40 percent of their population to go to church, even if it was Easter Sunday. And I have been in towns where there were church buildings on every corner.

All of my attempts to research information that will produce accurate and scientific data and statistics from clergy and congregations are like nailing Jell-o to a tree. In fact, a study conducted in the late 1990s by sociologist Stanley Presser, of the University of Maryland, and research assistant Linda Stinson, of the U. S. Bureau of Labor Statistics, assessed church attendance by actual diary entries as opposed to responses to pollsters. This study suggested Americans might be lying about their churchgoing habits to pollsters. It pegged church attendance at only 26 percent of Americans. This would certainly make a huge difference, yet the numbers could be totally skewed.

Let's just say we *can* believe that 40 percent of Americans do, in fact, attend church. One thing is certain: as you go further down the generational ladder, the percentage of churchgoers declines significantly. The drop is from 52 percent of builders (those born before 1946) and seniors to only 36 percent of gen Xers. In fact, Team America Tracking System (www.teamericatracking.org) estimates that there are 195 million unchurched people in America. It goes on to report that the combined communicant member-ship in Protestant churches over the last ten years has declined 9.5 percent (4,498,242 people) while the coun-try's population has increased 11.4 percent (24,153,000 people). Evangelical churches have failed to gain an additional two percent of the population over the past 50 years. It also states, "No county in America has a greater percentage of churched persons today than a decade ago," and that, "Half of all churches last year did not add one new member through conversion growth." What does this mean for the *future* of the church, especially in light of research that reflects 80 percent of money given to congregations comes from people aged fifty-five and older?[3] It makes us beg the question: What will the church do when the money runs out?

I'm at that age (fifty-none-of-your-business) where as a rule I don't stay up late at night. Not too long ago I conducted the wedding for a distant family member. This wedding had very interesting DNA. One of my granddaughters and two of my grandsons were in the wedding as flower girl and ring bearers. Because fam-ily was involved, my son-in-law and daughter were also a part of this particular wedding. Well, the deal was that GG (Grandmother Georgia) and Grand Grand (that's me) were to take the grandchildren home after the wedding and baby sit.

Now I have done hundreds of weddings but have only attended two or three of the wedding receptions. (That's just one of my personal quirks!) Because the three grandchildren were in this particular wedding, pictures were going to be taken at the reception (of course all of the people at the wedding were dying to see our little darlings) and we *were* to take them to our house for the night, so we decided to go to the reception. I must admit, my body felt like it had to be at least 2 a.m. (it was just a little after 9 p.m.) when it was time for us to leave.

We loaded up the three grandchildren, the bags of clothes for each child, and those "modern day contraptions" (that grandparents never had to deal with when our kids were small and you need a degree in engineering to make work) they call "car seats," said our goodbyes, and left the huge crowd at this elaborate hotel. (By the way, there was another huge crowd of people at another reception in the room next door.) We finally got to our house, got the precious little ones inside, changed their clothes and got them ready for bed, when my wife noticed that we had forgotten the diapers for the baby.

So I changed, threw one of my extra-large tee shirts onto my six-year-old grandson, and headed back in to town to retrieve the much-needed diapers. By this time, it was around 11 or 11:30 p.m. We picked up the diapers, and then my grandson decided he was hungry. (He really wasn't hungry but wanted one of those despicable toys they put in those expensive happy-meal bags.)

So we had to take an alternate route home. On our way to the burger place (that I thought should be fined for staying open so late), we drove by one of the local taverns. In the parking lot, as big a parking lot as you would find at Wal-Mart, they were having an outdoor dance with live music, flashy lights and all the trimmings, obviously including an endless supply of alcoholic beverages. I could not believe my eyes! I thought to myself, "If all *those* folks and the ones at the two wedding receptions would go to church tomorrow morning, churches all over the city would set new all-time high attendance records!

I thought to myself, "I bet that not many of those folks will be in church tomorrow." The point I'm making is that these people do not see the church as a vital part of their spiritual life. People *are* interested in searching for God and for personal salvation through a relationship with Him. They are *not*, however, turning to institutional religion for help with their search. In fact, just the opposite is true. They do not trust religious institutions because they see them as inherently self-serving. So off they go on their own search for God. But do not just take my word!

A 2001 survey in the *Christian Monitor* reported that the number of Americans who have "no religious preference" has doubled from 1990 to 2001, reaching 14 percent of the population. These are not skeptics; only one percent identified themselves as atheists.

George Barna reported in his book, *State of the Church*, that the unchurched population has grown from 24 to 34 percent in just one decade! Barna defines people as "unchurched" if they have not attended a Christian church service during the past six months, other than for special events such as weddings or funerals. Among some subgroups, the increase is even more substantial. Since 1991, the number of unchurched women has risen from 18 to 30 percent. The number of unchurched Hispanics has jumped from 19 percent to 33 percent. The number of unchurched people in the Northeast is up from 26 to 38 percent. The population of unchurched people on the West Coast has risen from 29 to 40 percent! (I live in Washington and work out of Seattle; Washington State is among the most unchurched states in the nation. Washington also has fewer churches than any other state.)

What about the retention rates? Dawson McAlister, national youth ministry specialist, says that 90 percent of kids active in high school youth groups do not go to church by the time they are sophomores in college. One-third of these students will never return. This rate of disconnection indicates a dilemma far more serious than mere youthful rebellion.

Let's take a short glance at a few of the realities outside the "church walls." *Ministries Today* reports that the divorce rate has risen 279 percent in the last 27 years. An ABC broadcast reports that the divorce rate in the "Bible Belt" is 50 percent higher than in other areas of the country. The Christian-based Barna Research Group reported in January 2000 that 21 percent of atheists and agnostics will or have experienced divorce, while 29 percent of Baptists and 34 percent of non-denominational Christians will or have experienced divorce. The average rate for all Christian groups is 27 percent.[4]

The point of all of this, at least in the eyes of this author, is proof that rugged and difficult times for pastors and ministries are upon us. The need for encouragement and affirmation for those who face the battle on the front lines is obviously apparent. One pastor recently wrote to me and said:

There is a need in our movement for some

"inspiring" meetings that will challenge all of us, especially those who have gone through some battles. Those of us who have faced some trials do not need to be a part of any more battles, but we need a place where we can heal, get challenged and really see God's face. I will now speak from the heart (very personal) and please accept it that way. In the past two years I have been abandoned by my wife, abandoned and lied about by my former church, and even abandoned by some of my friends. I, like others with like circumstances, need to be inspired and loved and challenged.

The current crisis in the environment of ministry is also affecting the wives and children of pastors, who get the spillover from the contamination that occurs in ministry today. One frightening statistic that brings tears to my eyes every time I share it with pastors and churches is that eighty percent of adult children of pastors surveyed will have to seek professional help for depression.

Eighty percent of the wives felt extreme pressures to be role models for the whole church. When asked if they were very satisfied with their marriage, 55 percent of the pastors said "yes." But when the wives were asked if they were *very* satisfied with their married life, only 25 percent said they were *very* satisfied with their family life. Eighty percent of pastors' spouses wish their spouse would choose another profession.

Eighty percent of pastors' wives feel pressured to do things and be something in the church that they really are not. The majority of pastors' wives surveyed said that the most destructive event that has occurred in their marriage and family was the day they entered the ministry. Eighty percent of pastors' wives feel left out and unappreciated by the church members.

I will never forget the day I was in a small town in Arkansas, sitting in the home of a pastor and his wife. The pastor's family had their "glass house" shattered by some hostile rocks thrown by some brutal, despicable and disgruntled people in their church. There I sat in the living room with the pastor and his lovely wife, tears flowing down all of our cheeks. She told me, "Dr. Pinion, if he does not leave the ministry, the kids and I are leaving him." To which he replied, "Brother, I do not know what else to do. I have been trained in ministry and have spent the last fifteen years in that profession. I have no other skills, talents or abilities to do anything *but* ministry."

When pastors' wives were surveyed and asked what the greatest challenge to their life was, they answered, "isolation and loneliness." The second challenge they indicated was, "limited time with their spouse" and that they "did not know how to manage it." The third challenge was "high expectations from the congregation." The demands of the ministry were so great that they "did not know how to do deal with it." A pastor in a small Arkansas town recently told me in a phone conversation, "We have seriously thought about getting out of the ministry. My wife does not know how much longer she can endure."

This book is written in hopes that pastors, their wives and their families, as well as the leadership of their congregations and their churches, will be informed, educated and made aware of the reality facing pastors, staff and missionaries across this nation and on foreign fields around the world.

Chapter 3

RATIONALE

You just don't understand!

Our deepest fear is not that we are inadequate. Our deepest fear is that we are powerful beyond measure. It is our light, not our darkness, that most frightens us. We ask ourselves, Who am I to be brilliant, gorgeous, talented and fabulous? Actually, who are you not to be? You are a child of God. Your playing small doesn't serve the world. There is nothing enlightened about shrinking so that other people won't feel insecure around you.

—Nelson Mandela

As I sit in a cabin in the mountains near McCall, Idaho, finishing this manuscript that I began nearly four years ago, I am surrounded by the most tranquil, picturesque and serene setting that a person could ever imagine. The last thing I thought I would experience, especially in this beautiful locale, would be the emotional "flashback" of the hurts in ministry I have personally experienced. Although it has been several years since I became one of the casualties of the church, I still feel some pain, hurt and even anger over what I experienced.

Today I can say that I *have* dealt with much of the bitterness I once felt as the result of "messy ministry," and I *have* risen above the past by allowing God's grace to heal my wounds and turn my experiences into a ministry for others.

This book is an attempt to show others that they are not the only ones who have been deeply injured by the abuse that hateful and disloyal layleaders and laypeople of the church have inflicted upon them.

In the pages that lie before you, I will be exposing some of the harsh realities "crushed clergy" have experienced. I do, however, want to say that most churches are full of wonderful and loving laypersons that care deeply for their pastor. The problems that I will be addressing are those caused by a very small percentage of persons. Yet these few individuals cause horrendous damage in the life of the church, the pastor and his family. This book is my attempt to provide encouragement, restoration, motivation and education to the abused and the abusers.

One pastor recently emailed me with his tragic and disheartened experience with "messy ministry." He said:

Five years ago this week I moved my family into a beautiful home in the Mid-South hoping for the pastoral experience that I would talk about for a lifetime. I had left one organization of churches for another looking for *"ministry at the next level."* We began with a 96 percent call, over a half a million dollars in the bank, a seemingly competent church staff and a pastoral search committee claiming, *"All this church needs is a good leader."* They boasted they had no problems in the church, and they were ready to build.

The Sunday evening of our candidacy, I was answering questions and I noticed one couple that seemed to have a *'barb'* in their words as they questioned me. We went to work through our honeymoon period and did our best to enable most of the 26 committees in the church. The former pastor had remained a part of the church and much of his family held key positions.

I was elected to the Vice Moderator position of our local churches and soon became chairman of their finance committee. Our church was standing room only, and we went to two services. Things were on a roll! Somewhere about that time, two or three of the 16 deacons began guerrilla warfare behind the scenes, second-guessing the few leadership moves we were making. After an incident on a trip with our youth, I found myself defending the action that had wisely been taken in correcting and training our student ministries director. Our two services were growing with regular decisions being made in the blended service and our offerings were spilling over into contingency accounts. Twenty-one months into our pastorate, I was asked at the end of the second service, while I was shaking hands, if I would go immediately to my office. There in my office were 21 men who were asking for my resignation by 5 PM that evening. If I were to do so then I would receive six months salary as severance. I called aside one of the men in the group who I thought was my friend (he was also the assistant chief of police of a large metropolitan city) and asked, "Why?" He could not give any reason, Biblical or otherwise, and was somewhat embarrassed to be part of the whole thing. Soon there was a confidence vote of my ministry and the church was very much divided. There were just enough votes to allow me to continue. The emotions were high and I asked our denomination to help us through a mediation process. For a year we bantered back and forth. The building fund had become a sacred cow and the $50,000 worth of architectural plans for a 600-seat sanctuary had become obsolete. We went on to remodel the existing chapel and watched as the people devoured one another. Today I sit begging God for another worthy ministry and some repair for my wife and children. It's almost comical to realize that 17 years ago, in graduate school, the theme I chose for my dissertation was, "The Evaluation and Suggested Designs for Coping in the Ministry." Who would have known!

I went by the church yesterday and someone had taken an old piece of sheet metal and screwed it to the beautiful lighted sign we had made. They hung a small piece of plywood on it and used Wal-Mart stick on lettering to advertise their service times. Some things never change.

Unfortunately, some things never do change! Of course, churches are human institutions, and they have been disappointing people since the time of Peter. I'm reminded of Paul's writings to young Timothy in II Timothy 4:9, 14, where he says, "Demas,

chasing fads, went off to Thessalonica and left me
here. . . . Watch out for Alexander the coppersmith.
Fiercely opposed to our Message, he caused no end of
trouble" (MSG).

Congregations, even during the earliest days of
the New Testament churches, experienced conflict
because of doctrinal disputes, personality differences,
leadership styles, moral values, personal and property
rights issues, sexuality, divorce, singleness, ministerial
authority, marriage for ministers, payment for
preachers, personal liberties in conduct, communion
practices, spiritual gifts, beliefs about resurrection of
the dead, special offerings, disciplinary practices,
hypocrisy, personal disagreements, disorderly conduct, laziness, gossiping and numerous unnamed
matters.

Dr. Paul Dixon, former president of Cedarville
University, who has preached in my pulpit when I was
pastoring and is as fine a Christian gentleman as you
could ever find, says that the church world is hardly
what many wish it to be. He once surveyed many of
the churches that supported the university. His
respondents, representing "hundreds of Bible-believ-
ing churches," reported that "twenty-five percent had
suffered major splits in their membership during the
previous five years. Another five percent said they

anticipated a significant division in the near future." Dr. Dixon, drawing from this data, concluded that, "The problems in the church are not primarily doctrinal or moral. They are, rather, brothers and sisters in Christ who have bitter, critical, unforgiving spirits."[1]

Wayne Kiser, following a study he conducted of 250 churches that experienced serious conflict, concluded that, "It is typically people perpetrated. Someone disagrees with the pastor, begins a quiet crusade among others in the congregation and forces the pastor to resign." Unfortunately, most pastors do not learn about a member's disagreement until it is too late.

A case in point was when one of my deacons came to me when I was pastoring and said that he had "several" people in the congregation coming to him with some complaints regarding me. I asked him how long this had been going on. His response was, "Several months now." I then asked him, "Have you told even one of the complainers to come and visit with me about their concerns?" They replied, "No." I then told him that *he* was in violation of the Scriptures for even listening to them (I Timothy 5:19) and for not having them come and talk with me (Matthew 18:15-16).

When I learned the identity of one of the men who was a catalyst for all the *lies* and *innuendos* that had been circulating, I asked him to come to my office.

When I confronted him with the matter, he began to yell and scream, "You are not feeding me and I have been at this church a lot longer than you and I have sure given a whole lot more money to this church than you and I'm not leaving!" I could not believe what I was hearing! Needless to say, that was the beginning of *my* "forced exit."

Even one of my most trusted men (at least I thought he was) made a phone call back to my former church, six years later, to find out why I left. Fortunately, the pastor of that church is a great friend of mine and he had the wisdom to ask the man, "If you haven't talked to Dr. Pinion, then don't think I will talk to you." And we wonder why so many pastors are getting burned out and leaving the ministry!

In the sunset of his seminary program, a pastoral intern was finally putting his book knowledge to practical use. With just a semester left before graduation, he had an epiphany: He was ready to chuck it all; his hope was dwarfed by disillusionment.

"He's wary because of the politics and conflict," said Eldon Fry, manager of pastoral care ministries for Focus on the Family, recalling a recent conversation he had with a concerned father-in-law. A few days later, Fry heard a similar story from another father whose young adult son informed him he was planning to leave the pastorate in several years to work with his dad in a landscaping business. "It's a sad thing to see young people burn out so quickly," said Fry, whose ministry includes a crisis line for clergy.[2]

Barney Self, a therapist with the Southern Baptist Convention's Leader Care Hot Line, which is operated by its LifeWay division, says, "Part of the problem is the notion that ministry is an obligation to be carried out by the paid staff. Pastors get absolutely inundated and deluged with the litany of responsibilities. They are taken advantage of."[3]

Dr. Michael Ross, a former pastor who left the ministry after finding himself overwhelmed by the details, and also a friend of mine to whom I have referred several pastors to at his pastor's institute, says, "What I found to be significant, but not surprising, was the amount of anger directed toward former co-pastors once a pastor leaves the profession. They feel abandoned, isolated and disconnected. Initial findings show that promises of better wages have little bearing on pastors leaving the ministry. They are leaving out of frustration, not out of the possibility of a new career or new opportunity. They do not see any possibility for change. They do not see the church being renewed. The best way out is to resign."

Dr. Ross credits the second biggest factor prompting pastors to leave as "disillusionment over the spiritual condition of their church." There is no longer a history within denominations. Most people joining churches are coming from other denominations. There is a subtle diffusion of the purpose of the church, the mission of the church and, therefore, the role of the pastor within the congregation."[4]

Doug Murren, in his book, *Churches That Heal, Becoming a Church That Mends Broken Hearts and Restores Shattered Lives,* says, "I have not always found church to be a friendly environment—neither as a young layperson nor as a pastor for nearly thirty years. As one friend of mine says, 'Doug, there's much in the church that is not in the Bible, and there is much in the Bible that is not in the church.' I have experienced betrayal; I have been misunderstood; I've been robbed; I have been libeled deliberately; I have felt so very alone in the midst of the fight—even as I was giving my all to the church. I have been bitter many times—convinced that the church no longer had much to offer me. In that, I have not been alone. I'm aware of many, many pastors and leaders who are cynical about the church. Some of the greatest betrayers I know are church members."[5]

A good pastor friend of mine sent me this email sharing his pain. He said:

I have had my share of 'ups and downs' in the ministry, but, after pastoring for over 25 years,

I never experienced anything that compares to being blindsided by two men in a church that I pastored for 12 years. After hearing rumors that some were wanting to get rid of me, I called those who were said to have made the statements. One of the men asked me to call a meeting to clear the air about a few things that had been going on in the church (a secretary that was messing around with a married guy in the church, *so I thought*). Little did I know what this secretary was up to, along with her sister (an associate's wife). The meeting started with me sharing my vision for the future and asking support for my dad whom I just found out had cancer. That support never came and the meeting ended with accusations of numerous things toward *me*. In other words, it was an attack on me and I had no clue, nor did any of the other men in the room. Only two men! There were three votes to get rid of us, but they never passed. Finally, after three months of pure hell, I resigned after a Sunday morning when I found out that another deacon had been swayed over. I realized what depression and fear are all about. I lost 35 pounds in three months. My wife stood by me and supported me, but she was also very hurt. My kids felt the same and the two at home experienced rebellion.

I suppose one of the most disheartening true life stories of "ministry messes" was from a pastor who wrote to say that a young man in his church, along with his family and another family, tried to get rid of him just like the four previous pastors. This young man stood up in the middle of his sermon and yelled, "Why don't you preach the truth?" After the service, the pastor confronted him; and, while they were talking, he continued to yell, "You liar!" People were standing around watching, so the pastor took him by the arm to usher him into his office. Three weeks later, the pastor was sued for $20,000 for assault and battery. He claimed the pastor put black and blue marks on his arm. It made headlines in the local newspaper and it dragged out for two years.

As this was going on, the pastor's youngest son and wife were expecting a baby. When the baby was born, he had some major physical problems. The pastor received an anonymous letter saying, "Isn't it a shame that a grandchild has to suffer for the sins of its grandfather?"

Why do *Christians* have to be so mean? Art Linkletter once said, "People don't get old and grouchy. They were young and grouchy and just got old." For example,

Montana's Matthew Shepard's grieving parents, while walking to his memorial service, had to pass by "Christians" waving signs. Matthew, a college student, had been beaten and murdered because he was gay. The signs did not say, "We're praying for you" or "Jesus will help heal your pain." The signs said things like "God hates fags." That was one of the nicer ones. When did Christians become some of the world's greatest haters? When did Christianity lose that over-the-top love for which the early Christians were most famous? What happened to, "They'll know we are Christians by our love"? Why do today's Christians love so badly?

We've all heard, "We are to *hate* the sin but *love* the sinner." Please! I'm afraid in today's church world there is far too much hatred going on and not enough love going out.

Why do churches seem to throw new believers into their "baby Christian incubators" immediately after they accept Christ as Savior, so they can, without delay, start "taking stands" for Jesus against this and against that?

Gary L. McIntosh & Samuel D. Rima, Sr., in their book, *Overcoming the Dark Side of Leadership,* give the following illustration:

> On arriving in Scotland, the American minis-
> ter and two of his church's board members

were anxious to meet their counterparts at a mission work they had been commissioned to visit. Coming, as they were, from a strong evangelical church in the States with a rich heritage in missions, the men were anxious to see what exciting things were being accomplished through the ministry of this church they were supporting. As they left their airport shuttle at the curb, they climbed the centuries-old stone stairs that led to the rectory. Before they could knock to announce their presence, the resident pastor flung open the door and with his arms fully extended in a grand gesture befitting a Eucharistic blessing, he enveloped the visitors in a warm embrace. *Ahh, the warmth of Christian fellowship extends even across the Atlantic,* thought the Yanks.

After appropriate hugs and greetings, the Scottish pastor ushered his guests into the wood-paneled comfort of the study and directed them toward ancient leather wingback chairs. It was an exciting occasion, one that called for a proper inauguration. The host reached for a richly grained wooden box that smelled of cedar. When he opened it, his guests saw a treasured store of choice cigars. With obvious pride, he offered each guest a cigar.

The two laymen nervously looked at one another, then gazed toward their own pastor, not quite sure of the proper protocol at such an awkward ceremony. With sullen faces belying more than a little disapproval, both laymen refused the offer. Their pastor, however, eagerly snared a cigar from the humidor and lit it up, appreciatively admiring the curl of thick smoke that rose to the beamed ceiling. The Scottish rector smiled with satisfaction.

Next, the Scot went to his credenza and collected from it four small glasses and an etched glass decanter containing a caramel-brown liquid. The laymen looked nauseous. Surely this was the reason that Christianity had died in the British Empire! When they returned home, they would see to it that the church reconsidered its financial support for such a carnal operation. They refused the brandy with even less decorum than they had rejected the cigars. Their host was by now looking worried, wondering if he had somehow done something wrong. The American pastor, to the chagrin of his traveling companions, once again accepted the offering and took a satisfying sip. After an hour of visiting, confirmation of the coming itinerary and a departing benediction, the Americans left. Once in their cab, the laymen wasted no time before launching into an interrogation of their pastor. "Pastor, how could you?" exclaimed one of the board members, "I thought we were here to support their ministry and encourage them in their evangelistic efforts—it's no wonder the church is dead over here!" After a moment of silence, the pastor replied, with more than a hint of disgust, "One of us had to act like a Christian."

What does it mean to act like a Christian? What are the legitimate, Biblical expectations placed on believers? Today many rank-and-file evangelicals would pronounce the behavior of the pastor in our apocryphal story highly suspect. Yet his actions may have been more consistent with the example of Christ, and his heart and motives more in tune with the Savior's.

God forbid that any pastor today would participate in a wedding party where alcohol was served, as Jesus did at Cana. He would quickly be accused of condoning sinful behavior; never mind what would be said if the pastor ran to the store to buy more wine when the family's supply ran low.[6]

Isn't it Jesus who gives us a "new life?" Isn't it

Jesus who makes the dead alive? Isn't it Jesus who turns our beings inside out and upside down? The body is the "temple of the Spirit." Your body is riddled with the sacred. Your body is suffused with divinity—the wild, vibrant energies of the sacred. And when you let that energy of the Spirit work within you, your mind, your body and your world *will* change.

Chapter 4

RESULTS

Where in the world are they going?

Strike the shepherd and the sheep will be scattered . . .
Zechariah 13:7

One pastor recently wrote to me saying:

Here is what has happened over the past year and a half at our church. As you know, we went through a building program. The work is complete! Thank God for that. The people really responded well through the program. The morale stayed very high, and the people gave very well. Soon after, a group of about 15-20 people began to stir things up, one of whom was my personal prayer partner. Well, it got real bad. They did finally leave, but about eight to 10 others took their place and refused to leave. For the past year they have really

knocked the wind out of our sails. All momen-
tum was lost. Most of these people have not
left. It was a situation that everyone knew was
going on and all the leaders knew it was wrong,
but it was not dealt with because the people
involved were very influential people. I nearly
walked away from everything I've committed
my life to doing. My wife and family took a
beating. We were very discouraged. I know that
God wants me to pastor. I love it with all my
heart, but I'm not sure how long we will stay.
While I have got the wind back in *my* sails, the
church has been slower to recover. I know that
I cannot personally turn it around. Although
our deacons and staff have begun to talk, I am
not really sure how willing they are to take a
stand and work through the hard things. Thus,
I have felt the need to call on you.

Another pastor and his family that
Encouragement Dynamics ministry had the privilege
and honor, through God's grace and wisdom, to help
wrote me saying:

My wife and I would like to thank you and
your ministry for helping us through a very
difficult time. Our first church was a church

with a history of conflict and a very low opinion
of pastors. However, God used us there for eight
years (longer than any pastor in the church's history). From the start, we faced resistance from
the owners of the church. But God started
bringing in new people and converts. We ended
up with two churches under one roof. One
group was very unreceptive and the other group
was growing in Christ enthusiastically. Some of
the old guard decided they could not wear me
out, so they finally started having secret meetings and calling for my dismissal.

I thought I could withstand their attack,
but they spread rumors and lies at a rapid
speed. I guess the conflict of eight years finally wore me out and I ended up having an emotional breakdown. I had nothing left to give.
Knowing that even though the majority wanted me to stay, yet one-third could vote me out,
I knew if I did stay it would be conflict riddled
and the old guard would be just as, if not more
so, resistant. I resigned in May and we have
been living out of our van for two months. We
will be going to a 'recovery' church in Denver
where I am supposed to be built back up in the
ministry and work outside of ministry until I
get my ability to minister back.

It was during my emotional breakdown that my wife searched the Internet to try to find someone to help me, since there really was no one we could turn to. She found your ministry on the Focus on the Family website. She sent you an e-mail and you immediately wrote her back with encouragement and hope. Then you called us and spoke with us for an hour, after you had a long day of seminars. We really appreciated that. What you had said to us kept us hopeful and helped us realize that there were many others who knew what we were going through. You helped get us connected with the appropriate caregivers at a special renewal retreat center, and we ended up going there for five days of counseling/encouragement.

I am still in the 'zombie' mode: not feeling much, not thinking much, just trying to get through the day. I do dread finding a secular job while I am at the 'recovery' church, but I don't feel I have anything to offer right now 'ministry' wise. I know God is in control and He is working all of this to conform my family and me to be more like Jesus (Romans 8:28-29). What others meant for evil, God will use for His glory. I am looking forward with anticipation to see what God actually has in store for us.

Thanks again for your help, for your counsel, and for getting us connected with others
who could minister to us. We have done so
much ministering to others, but so little ministering has been done to us. It is a little hard for
us to be the recipients. We need it; and still so
few are giving it. May the Lord bless you and
your ministry to Christ's under-shepherds.

"Enormous Loss of Pastors Reported," reads the
title to an article in *the Inland Northwest Christian News.*
The article says, "A report, by Dr. Sam Logan, presented at the annual meeting of the Fellowship of
Evangelical Seminary Presidents (FESP), indicates
pastors in the United States are 'dropping like flies.'
There is an incredible dropout rate. FESP met in
Coronado, California, January 2 through 4, 2003.
Included was a survey from Focus on the Family that
indicates, on the average, across the country and
across all denominations, 1,800 ministers leave the
ministry *every month*! In other words, 21,600 pastors a
year—an attrition rate of two to three an hour. What
are churches doing to drive away the shepherds? Less
obvious, though, is the fact that more ministers are
leaving the ministry than all United States accredited
seminaries combined are replacing! Significantly,
church buildings could sit empty, be boarded up, or

be turned into commercial property. A bulwark seg-
ment of American society and history, possibly even
American architecture, may be vanishing and is, at
least, on the endangered species list."[1]

On June 10, 2005, the Pastoral Advocacy Network
of San Diego, California, estimated that approximate-
ly 1,000 ministers per week were being rejected from
the ministry, or were choosing to leave for self-preser-
vation reasons, in hope of finding a life with less personal stress. They go on to say, "Pastors are leaving the
ministry for a variety of reasons: most have experienced great disrespect, personal attacks, forced termination, or public humiliation at the hands of unruly
church-goers."

When preaching from the Bible is met with a lack of
willingness to listen to God's servant, when rebellion is
thought of as being helpful, when a conspiracy of evil is
thought to be the voice of reason and righteousness,
when everything honest and good in the character of
the minister is twisted into vice and sin, it creates
immense discouragement that makes one want to
throw in the proverbial towel and take the first and
quickest exit. One writer described the feeling as true
persecution, or to state it another way, it's "soul cruci-
fixion" and "acute pastor abuse." The *Los Angeles Times*
printed a special report that stated, "People are leaving
the ministry in droves because it's too difficult."

In the nearly 30 years of ministry that I have had the privilege to serve as a pastor myself, radical changes and unreasonable expectations have taken root that catapult this great exodus. The pastoral role moved from simple shepherding to being CEO, CFO, resident lawyer, visionary, program manager, God's perfect counselor on all matters, fidelity fixer, facilities superintendent, perpetual committee member, human resources director, successful fundraiser, par excellent communicator, career advisor, marketing supervisor, politician, spiritual example, masterful preacher, artful teacher, community leader, welfare administrator, contractor, organizational appeaser and, too often, people-pleaser. Ah, and oh yes: perfect spouse and perfect parent with perfect children in the perfect home.

If you remove one pastor and cause a church to scatter, then another and yet another, it will not take long for corruption to creep in and seize the land. As I alluded to earlier in this book, there *are* times when it really *is* best for a pastor to step down. Yet, far too many good pastors are being driven out of ministry, leaving thousands of churches weak and vulnerable to spiritual attack. Without healthy pastor/shepherds leading the flocks, factions multiply, evangelism declines, divorces proceed unimpeded, discipleship loses direction, and missionaries are forgotten on the field.

A study by the Barna Research Group, which does marketing studies of American culture and the Christian faith, found that, whereas 20 years ago the average minister remained at least seven years in his parish, today his stay has eroded to barely five years. Barna's research, conducted between July 2000 and June 2001, was based on a survey of 1,865 senior pastors of Protestant churches nationwide. This trend, George Barna warns, "may be shortchanging pastors—and the congregations they oversee—by prematurely terminating their tenure."

Rabbi Joel Meyers, executive vice president of the Conservative Rabbinical Assembly, acknowledges that 30 percent of rabbis who changed positions in 2000 did so because they were forced to leave their congregations.

Similarly, Marcia Myers, director of personnel services for the Presbyterian Church (USA), reports that of the 84 cases in which relations were ended in 2000, one-fourth were involuntary.

To give some context to these numbers, Kevin Leicht, professor of sociology at the University of Iowa and author of *Professional Work*, says, "Clergy firings are very high compared with the national labor force, where 1.2 percent of all employees are involuntarily terminated. The rate is even higher than coaches in the NFL, a notoriously unstable profession." This uprooting comes with costs to both the church and its minister: "Most grievous is the trauma to the minister, who must dislodge his family and leave town."

George Barna noted that many pastors are not given an adequate opportunity to shine. "Our work has found that the typical pastor has his or her greatest ministry impact at a church in years five through fourteen of their pastorate. Unfortunately, we also know that the average pastor lasts only five years at a church—forfeiting the fruit of their investment in the church they have pastored. In our fast turnaround society where we demand overnight results and consider everyone expendable and everything disposable, we may be shortchanging pastors—and the congregations they oversee—by prematurely terminating their tenure."

For the good of the congregation and clergy, more aggressive strategies are needed to halt this trend. A separate study by church consultant Alan Klaas, president of Mission Growth Ministries, investigated the causes of ousters in various Christian denominations. In the study, he tried to find the source of the problem and where opportunities for reforms exist. The report put most of the blame on the congregation:

> In 67 percent of the cases, the congregation had been in conflict with the previous pastor too. In 45 percent of the cases, a minority

faction was successful in manipulating a supportive majority to push the pastor out. Only seven percent of the time was the cause the personal misconduct of the minister. Sadly for all, in 62 percent of the cases, regional officials of these various denominations who could have helped mediate were kept away until it was too late to solve the dispute.

A study by my good friend Charles H. Chandler, who is the executive director for the Ministering to Ministers Foundation, noted that pastors who have been forcibly terminated reveal some interesting dynamics:

> After facilitating a session of participants' stories at a Healthy Transitions Wellness Retreat, I was asked, "Is there a rulebook on forced termination?" He had observed similar "dynamics" or "rules" in the stories. At every retreat, the participants are amazed at the similarities in the forced termination experience.
>
> Several years ago, the psychiatrist assisting with a retreat was appalled as he heard the stories. He worked extensively with corporations in "downsizing" and noted that none of them treated employees like the

churches treated the retreat participants. He observed three "dynamic" patterns in all of their stories.

First, each minister had been "blind-sided." A group of two or three persons, usually self-appointed, approached the minister without warning and said he/she should resign because of loss of effectiveness. They convinced the minister that the whole church shared their feeling. The group presented themselves as merely messengers and insisted there was nothing personal about the request. The messengers told the minister they loved him/her and really hated to deliver the resignation request.

Second, while the minister was in a state of shock after being "blind-sided," the "group" dumped guilt on the minister. They said the resignation and related conversation must be kept very quiet. If word got out, it could split the church. And, the minister would not want to be known as one who caused a split church! Any negative effect from the minister's leaving was dumped directly on him/her as though a minister could just slip away and never be missed.

Third, while the minister was still in no

condition to make a decision of any kind, the group pressed for a decision. In most cases, a few weeks or a few months of severance was offered—provided the resignation was given immediately and the entire conversation kept quiet.

The messengers added, "We have to know what you plan to do, because if you refuse to resign or if you talk to other church members, we will take away the severance and call a church business meeting to fire you. Then you will get nothing."

Again, the minister was told there was nothing personal about the request. They had to do what was best for the church. No reasons were given for the forced termination except that the church needed new, more effective leadership.

I have worked with hundreds of ministers who have experienced forced termination. At this point, I have decided a rulebook is floating around out there somewhere and it does suggest that a few disgruntled church members can follow the above listed rules and "kick the preacher out." I've never seen it in writing, but its effectiveness can be seen in case after case.

Look with me at some of the fallacies and undesirable ethics endorsed by this phantom rulebook.

Though the messengers present themselves as representing the vast majority of the membership, according to a survey conducted by *Leadership* magazine, 43 percent of forced-out ministers said a "faction" pushed them out, and 71 percent of those stated that the "faction" numbered 10 persons or less. The self-appointed messengers often horde the inside information, because only 20 percent of the forced out ministers said the real reason for their leaving was made known to the entire congregation.

Frequently, the decision is made by an informal clique without authority. And, I am convinced, the statement telling the minister to remain quiet or risk losing severance money translates, "We do not have the votes to remove the minister via a church vote."

Ministers often remain quiet because they are afraid to take a chance on having nothing with which to house and feed their families. A significant number of ministers have no savings due to inadequate salaries. They often fall victim to the group's argument that remaining quiet is taking the "high road."

Remaining quiet also creates dynamics that make it easy for the church to become a repeat-offender church. The next time a small but vocal group is dissatisfied with the minister, the same old rulebook is consulted and another minister is forced out. Disclosing the secret may be painful, but it is the only way a church is able to stay or become healthy.

As much consideration should be given to leaving a position as is given to accepting a position. Otherwise, the Lord's leadership has little opportunity to guide the process. A minister does not owe a self-appointed "faction" an on-the-spot answer. Time for prayer and processing with confidants or mentors is vital. Certainly, ministers have the right to take adequate time for healthy decision making.

The bottom line, as I see it, in dealing with the forced termination process is clear-cut and well defined. Written or unwritten effective rules or dynamics are in place to force a minister out. However, this process is done in secret and without proper notification or concern.[2]

I believe if we lose our leaders, we lose our churches. And if we lose our churches, we lose our communities.

And if we lose our communities, we will lose our world!

The reasons for stress, burnout and discouragement among ministers may be as numerous and unique as there are pastors. However, recent research is unanimous in citing the following problem areas: the disparity between expectations and hard reality; lack of clearly defined boundaries—tasks are never done; workaholism; the "Peter Principle"—feeling of incompetence in leading an army of volunteers; conflict in being a leader and servant at the same time; intangibility—how do I know I'm getting somewhere? Additional problem areas include: confusion of role identity with self image—pastors derive too much self-esteem from what they do; time management problems (yet pastors have more 'discretionary time' than any other professional group); paucity of "perks"; multiplicity of roles; inability to produce "win-win" conflict resolutions; difficulty in managing interruptions; clergy are too serious, they have difficulty being spontaneous; preoccupation with "playing it safe" to avoid enraging powerful parishioners; "administration overload"—too much energy expended in areas of low reward; and loneliness—the pastor is less likely to have a close friend than any other person in the community.

An article in *Northwest Christian Times* by Lori Arnold says, "Young or old, pastors are feeling the burden as they juggle the responsibilities of shepherd, counselor, building superintendent, marketer, cheerleader, teacher and disciplinarian."

George Barna, president of Barna Research Group in Oxnard, California, in one of his surveys found research that suggested, "To appreciate the contribution made by pastors, you have to understand their world and the challenges they face. Our studies show that churchgoers expect their pastor to juggle an average of 16 major tasks. That's a recipe for failure—nobody can handle the wide range of responsibilities that people expect pastors to master." He goes on to say, "Being a pastor these days may be the single most thankless task in America. National surveys indicate that people are less likely to trust and to be influenced by clergy than used to be the case, and that pastors themselves are increasingly frustrated in ministry. As our culture becomes more complex and people's needs become more challenging, the quality of pastoral leadership is one of the most significant indicators of the current health and potential influence of the Church in America."

Mr. Barna continues by saying, "Most pastors work long hours, are constantly on-call, often sacrifice time with family to tend to congregational crises, carry long-term debt from the cost of seminary and receive below-average compensation in return for performing a difficult job. Trained in theology, they are expected to master leadership, politics, finance, management, psychology and conflict resolution. Pastoring must be a calling from God if one is to garner a sense of satisfaction and maintain unflagging commitment to that job."

Dr. Dan Rieland of Injoy ministries says, "Pastors, particularly senior pastors, are often seen as an unrealistic combination of the Apostle Paul and Billy Graham or perhaps Rambo and 007 ...whatever fits best! The point is, the perception is unrealistic—and often superhuman." Their lives are played out in a fishbowl, with the entire congregation and community watching their every move. They are expected to have ideal families, to be perfect people, to always be available, to never be down and to have all the answers we need in order to keep our own lives stable and moving forward. Those are unrealistic expectations to place on anyone, yet most of us are disappointed when a pastor becomes overwhelmed, seems depressed, lets us down or completely burns out. And we certainly never blame ourselves for their "failures."

Spiritual leaders are prime targets in these last days. The Bible tells us that if you strike a shepherd, the sheep will scatter. Entire congregations can be wiped out with a single blow to one shepherd. For this reason they are the number one public enemy on

Satan's hit list. Like the classic "Far Side" cartoon, pastors are born again with an unfortunate bull's eye shaped birthmark emblazoned on their back. It is constantly sought out by the powers of darkness. Corresponding with this gigantic loss of shepherds, new studies are also providing growing evidence of a great loss of churches. A study in *Exit Interviews* by Hendricks shows the appalling results of the loss of ministers: there are now 53,000 people leaving churches weekly who are not coming back. George Barna's research sadly declares that we are losing one percent of our churches in America every year, as godly warriors depart from the battle arena. As shepherds leave, sheep leave.

One lady dealing with the "fallout" of her pastor wrote the following. She said, "The conflict resulted in the pastor being forced to leave. Because of this decision, the people who supported the pastor left the church. The church attendance was reduced to half, relationships were severed, weekly income was drastically cut, and various ministries in the church were forced to disband. The church became known in the community as a place of power struggles, fighting and discontent. I could go on and on."[3]

"Pastors are the single most occupationally frustrated group in America," says Southern California psychologist Richard Blackmon, quoted in a Los Angeles Times story on the demands faced by today's spiritual leaders. "Roughly 30 percent to 40 percent of religious leaders eventually drop out of the ministry," according to Blackmon. "About 75 percent go through a period of stress so great that they consider quitting. The incidence of mental breakdown is so high that insurance companies charge about four percent extra to cover church staff members when compared to employees in other businesses."[4]

A pastor from Ventura, California, said, "I could empathize with my friend, a 55-year-old pastor who ran away from his congregation a week ago and spent three nights wandering the snow-covered mountains in San Diego County." When found, he told authorities he was overwhelmed by life and just needed to get away. The demand to be on-call for a congregation 24 hours a day—as personal confidant, marriage counselor, crisis interventionist—puts church leaders in a constant whirlwind of stressful events, says the article. And when the phone rings, a pastor is expected to answer the call no matter how tired or strained he may feel.

The profession is often characterized as more stress-ridden than that of a doctor dealing with a terminal illness, since the doctor can walk away from the situation when he leaves the room. The pastor, however, unlike other professionals, normally has emotional links and personal ties to those being helped and suffers with them.

Congregations and communities place additional pressure on ministers, smothering them with intense scrutiny and expecting them to conduct lives far more holy than their own. Additionally, religious leaders, especially those heading up small churches, wear several administrative hats—worrying about attendance, bills, building repairs, staffing issues and volunteer recruitment—on top of preparing multiple sermons, messages and Bible lessons each week. "Their strong religious beliefs mean they will not kill themselves," says pastoral psychologist Archibald Hart. "They just spend their time wishing they were dead."[5]

Chapter 5

RECONCILIATION

A refuge amidst the storm!

One of the most insidious maladies of our time [is]: the tendency in most of us to observe rather than act, avoid rather than participate, not do rather than do; the tendency to give in to the sly, negative, cautionary voices that constantly counsel us to be careful, to be controlled, to be wary and prudent and hesitant and guarded in our approach of this complicated thing called living.
—Arthur Gordon, *A Touch of Wonder*

A major part of the problem is that the North American Church is largely patterned after secular models of leadership. Goals, strategies and performance have by and large replaced relationship, caring and friendship in church leadership.

That's all fine as long as we are working on a ministry project or raising money, but when a life is hurt along the way, the secular model of leadership cannot deliver God's healing grace. Churches must make the relationship among its leaders a central priority, so that when a pastor or other leader enters deep water, there is more to fall back on than just a budget or performance review. Pastors need the safety net of relationship and friendship to fall into when things head south.

How do you measure the productivity of ministry? How do you measure a minister's worth? What do you consider when attempting to "evaluate" how good or bad a pastor is doing? Are ministers to be measured by their skills, education and achievements? Are they to be gauged by human terms like "getting the job done?" Are they to be assessed by how much time they spend in the office or out of the office?

The great prophet Ezekiel had a message for Israel. He was to do nothing but lay around on his left side for 390 days, then lay another 40 days on his right side, while eating dung (Ezekiel 4:4-6). How do you measure his pastoring skills? According to 2 Peter 2:5, Noah was a righteous preacher, yet he had no converts after 100 years of preaching. Was he a bad preacher? Jonah refused to take the message of God to Nineveh and only reluctantly spoke it after landing on its shores, courtesy of a nauseous whale, with God's ultimatum. After his nation-saving sermon, he sat under a tree—regretting his action and angry with God.

Would you consider him to be an accomplished spiritual leader? Yet, these three—the lazy, crazy prophet, the zookeeper/desert boat builder, and the whining coward—are considered giants in the Kingdom of God.

Could it be that our method of judging spiritual leaders is flawed? Could it be that we are judging spiritual leaders on the scales of human secular and corporate understanding? Has the methodology of corporate evaluation replaced the wisdom unveiled by spiritual discernment? My experience is that the deplorable treatment of the Lord's shepherds saddens God, even angers Him. These servants and their message are being rejected, much like the Old Testament prophets just before the Captivity.

"Now we ask you, brothers, to respect those who work hard among you, who are over you in the Lord and who admonish you. Hold them in the highest regard in love because of their work. Live in peace with each other" (I Thessalonians 5:12-13, NIV). "Remember your leaders, who spoke the Word of God to you. Consider the outcome of their way of life and imitate their faith" (Hebrews 13:7, NIV). If we obeyed just these two simple verses to the fullest, we would see a dramatic revival, both in the lives of pastors and in our churches!

I believe the treatment of pastors in America today is at a crisis level. I believe that it is critical that we

rediscover restoration and reconciliation, and re-
investing honor in the gift of shepherding. Bill
Hybels, in his book *Courageous Leadership*, said, "The
local church is the hope of the world and its future
rests primarily in the hands of its leaders. As our culture becomes more complex and people's needs
become more challenging, the quality of pastoral
leadership is one of the most significant indicators of
the current health and potential influence of the
Church in America."

As stated earlier, my fear is that if we lose our leaders, we lose our churches. If we lose our churches, we
lose our communities. If we lose our communities, we
lose our world.

This nation has aligned itself with the works of
darkness and has become so adept at tearing down
that it has misplaced its tools of building up. The
rebuilding must begin at home with the family. It is
in these incubation chambers of society—the living
rooms, kitchens and bedrooms of the saints—that
true respect for shepherds is nurtured. Here, the Holy
Spirit has His most profound influence. What goes
on behind these closed doors determines the effectiveness of church leadership. For it is behind the
cloistered walls of private homes that either the most
stinging condemnation or the most precious aromat-
ic fragrance of blessing toward the shepherds of God's

Kingdom takes place. It is either the labor room of gossip or the "ground zero" of honor.

We must flee gossip, scandal and caustic chitchat; it does not edify but tears down. When this happens, we will see a renewed shaping of human lives into great men and women of God who highly respect God's called leaders.

I Timothy 5:17 says, "Let the elders who rule well be considered worthy of double honor, especially those who work hard at preaching and teaching" (NAS).

Before we understand double honor, it might be wise to define honor. Honor in its purest form means "recognizing God and others as more significant than your self." Such honor glorifies God. It is what God intends to exist in the church. More than one person's ministry has persevered through adversity because of honor received.

Honor sometimes comes from the most unlikely sources. I have received hundreds of cards and letters during my years as a senior pastor. Some have been extremely hateful and hurtful. (I always made it a practice *not* to open or even read any letter with no signature. I felt that if the person writing the letter did not have enough character to sign it then it was not worth my time to read it.) Others have been encouraging, edifying and affirming. Some of the most precious and endearing have come from children. One in particular was from a little girl who could not even spell "pastor" but said, "You are the best 'pasture' in the world. You make me laugh! Thanks for being my 'pasture.' I love you!"

Nothing is more rewarding than kind words spoken in response to one's ministry. "A word fitly spoken is like apples of gold in pictures of silver" (Proverbs 25:11).

We see so little honor in our society that disrespect reins in our homes, churches, sports, politics and the corporate world. Living examples of honoring others have all but vanished. The meaning of the word is discovered when we place high value on someone or something, treasuring it as our most valuable possession. After careful consideration, we should choose to place the highest degree of respect on the man of God and reverence him.

Respect means to give favorable regard to a person and to refrain from interfering with them. *Reverence* is shown by displaying tenderness of feeling with a profound admiration for someone. You deem them worthy of your finest thoughts and actions. In sincerity and simplicity, you determine them to be deserving people, worthy of your care and concern, for they are gifts sent from God to guide you to the Savior of your soul. It is a matter of the heart first and foremost.

Now that you have a picture of what it means to honor a shepherd in your heart, double it and you will come close to God's definition of double honor. Do twice as much as you are planning now. You cannot respect His shepherds enough.

Verse seventeen especially indicates that double honor is to go to those who work hard at preaching and teaching. The shepherd's value is in their *gift*, not in their *achievements*.

As the book of Acts indicates, everything possible must be done to eliminate any burden from the shoulders of the shepherd, except prayer and the ministry of the Word. With all the expectations placed on pastors today, something has to give! Usually that which is neglected is that which should be prioritized: prayer and the ministry of the Word! People must shift their expectations of pastors and stop expecting them to be "jacks of all trades" and directors of the church corporation.

At the same time, God's people should raise their expectations of the shepherd in spiritual matters. Wouldn't it be amazing to find your pastor on his face before God interceding for you, instead of disturbing him out of his numerous staff and business meetings?

After true respect has been restored to your heart by the Holy Spirit, there are endless things that you can do to show your respect

Double honor does have its price. The price is

opening your heart to God and closing your mouth
(and thoughts) to criticism. It also may force you to
slaughter and barbeque some of the "sacred cows" of
your traditions.

Another critical part of reconciliation is creating
an environment in our churches that will accommodate healing. We have all heard the cliché, "The
church is not a hotel for the saints but a hospital for
sinners." But do we really believe it?

President Bush recently commended pro-life
activists, saying that they were "helping to create a culture of life." The church, also, needs to become a culture of life—a place where life is nurtured, loved and
healed. In centuries past, a primary metaphor for the
church was the "hospital of the soul"; it was expected to
be a safe place for hurting, broken people.
Unfortunately, the contemporary "board room" model
of the church offers little hope to hurting pastors or
congregants. Church lay leaders and pastors must
once again adopt the hospital metaphor for the
church. It would then have a proper identity out of
which to extend healing and reconciliation to one
another—including their wounded, discouraged,
depressed and burned out pastor.

Another critical component in reconciliation is
accountability. I never have been high on "accountability" because accountability is only as good as the

character of the one who is being held accountable. Most people also forget that accountability is a two-way street.

I do, however, like what E. Glen Wagner said in an article he wrote for *REV* magazine: "Walking Alone: My Journey Into Depression." He wrote, "A lot of thought is being given to the place and practice of pastoral accountability. By accountability, most churches have in mind a process that resembles an IRS audit. The pastor's performance is assessed. His sermons are critiqued. Is he drawing in new members? Is he meeting his goals? Is there anything about him we do not like? Should we 'retain him as our pastor?' (A phrase actually used in many pastoral reviews). This kind of performance-based accountability fuels depression and needs to be improved."

He suggests, "What pastors need is mutuality. Pastors need quality feedback that includes encouragement and constructive criticism. By and large, pastors receive little encouragement from their lay leaders and church members and receive much constructive criticism—which is a big reason so many of us are depressed."

He goes on to say, "But pastors also need to insist on the opportunity to affirm and evaluate the church and how it's doing in supporting his ministry. This would allow for early detection of relational problems that could become sources of depression and discouragement if left unaddressed. And leaders need to have the courage to deal with it."

The bad news is that your pastor, like pastors everywhere, is at risk of becoming just another statistic. He is expected to do so much, be so much, and give so much that many times there is nothing left for him. We, the church, cannot afford to keep losing pastors to burnout and contention. Think about it!

Chapter 6

RECOVERY

It'll feel better when it quits hurting!

I will not leave you alone. You are mine. I know each of My sheep by name. You belong to Me. If you think I am finished with you, if you think I am a small god that you can keep at a safe distance, I will pounce upon you like a roaring lion, tear you to pieces, rip you to shreds, and break every bone in your body. Then I will mend you, cradle you in my arms, and kiss you tenderly.

—Brennan Manning, *Lion and Lamb*

I know that I have painted a pretty dismal and gloomy picture of the ministry and the church. But the good news is that many of the stories that I have shared have one thing in common. The commonality is that most wounded pastors have recognized that all the negatives and painful circumstances have helped determine their future. They have moved from bitterness to acceptance to openness to effectiveness. They have learned that until you have *hurt*, you will not be able to *help* the hurting.

Pain, if you will let it, will teach you to see what is really important in a way success never can.

THE ROAD OF LIFE

At first, I saw God as my observer, my judge, keeping track of the things I did wrong, so as to know whether I merited heaven or hell when I die.

He was out there sort of like a president. I recognized His picture when I saw it, but I really didn't know Him.

But later on when I met Christ, it seemed as though life was rather like a bike ride, but it was a tandem bike, and I noticed that Christ was in the back helping me pedal.

I do not know just when it was that He suggested we change places, but life has not been the same since.

When I had control, I knew the way. It was rather boring, but predictable. It was the shortest distance between two points.

But when He took the lead, He knew delightful long cuts, up mountains and through rocky places at breakneck speeds; it was all I could do to hang on!

Even though it looked like madness, He said, "Pedal!" I worried and was anxious and asked, "Where are you taking me?"

He laughed and did not answer and I started to learn to trust.

I forgot my boring life and entered into the adventure. And when I'd say, "I'm scared," He'd lean back and touch my hand.

He took me to people with gifts that I needed, gifts of healing, acceptance and joy.

They gave me gifts to take on my journey, my Lord's and mine.

And we were off again. He said, "Give the gifts away; they are extra baggage, too much weight."

So I did, to the people we met, and I found that in giving I received, and still our burden was light.

I did not trust Him at first, in control of my life. I thought He would wreck it; but He knows bike secrets, knows how to make it bend to take sharp corners, knows how to jump to clear high rocks, knows how to fly to shorten scary passages.

And I am learning to shut up and pedal in the strangest places, and I am beginning to enjoy the view and the cool breeze on my face with my delightful constant companion, Jesus Christ.

And when I am sure I just cannot do anymore, He just smiles and says. . . "PEDAL."

Pedal on! The best is yet to come!

I have discovered that God can use my woundedness as a pastor to become a wounded healer for other beaten, broken, bruised and battered pastors across this nation. An anonymous person once said, "A word of encouragement during failure is worth more than an hour of praise after success."

Some careful observers who have studied the fall-out from wounded pastors, as well as the dilemma that faces many of our churches all across the nation, are calling this problem "epidemic." Lloyd Rediger begins his study of this crisis as follows:

> Abuse of pastors by congregations and the breakdown of pastors due to inadequate support are tragic realities. This worst-case scenario for the church, one that is increasing in epidemic proportions, is not a misinterpretation by a few discontented clergy. Rather, it is a phenomenon that is verified by both research and experience.

So what are major church leaders doing about this tragedy? Rediger continues:

> Worse yet, there is a strong tendency toward denial of this reality in denominational offices and among clergy who have not yet been forced out of their congregations or battered emotionally and spiritually while trying to be faithful pastors.[1]

Denial or underestimation of the problem by those who should know better and who are in a position to do something about it means that the only ones left in a position to do something constructive and redemptive about the problem are those pastors who have personally experienced the pain. These are the ones who are uniquely experienced to become wounded healers of the afflicted.

The concept of a wounded healer came several years ago from Henri J. M. Nouwen, a Roman Catholic scholar, who was then teaching at Yale Divinity School. His book, *The Wounded Healer,* is now a classic. The title was suggested in an old legend Nouwen found in the Talmud, the collection of ancient rabbinic writings that make up the basis of religious authority for traditional Judaism. The legend is this:

> Rabbi Yoshua ben Levi came upon Elijah the prophet while he was standing at the entrance of Rabbi Simeron ben Yohai's cave . . . He asked Elijah, "When will the Messiah come?"
>
> Elijah replied, "Go and ask him yourself."
>
> "Where is he?"
>
> "Sitting at the gates of the city."
>
> "How shall I know him?"
>
> "He is sitting among the poor covered with wounds. The others unbind all their wounds at the same time and then bind them up again.

But he unbinds one at a time and binds it up again, saying to himself, 'Perhaps I shall be needed; if so I must always be ready so as not to delay for a moment.'"[2]

The story reveals that the Messiah is to be found among the poor, needy and injured, binding his own wounds one at a time, anticipating the moment when his healing care will be needed. So it can be with wounded ministers who are trying to grow spiritually and emotionally through their experiences of pain. They must look after their own wounds, but at the same time be ready to offer healing support to other wounded ministers.

The hurts and pain you experienced can be filled with purpose and meaning as you reach out to other wounded ministers to help heal their injured spirits. It actually facilitates your own healing when you take your eyes off yourself and focus on the injuries of others in the ministry.

Encouragement Dynamics ministry is a part of a network of "caregivers" across the nation. Most who have crossed over the Red Sea of horrific experiences and labor pains give birth to phenomenal ministries that help others. These men and women have experienced the love, mercy, grace and forgiveness of Christ and are willing to pass on their stories in hope of restoring health to the hurt, wounded and discouraged.

A great example of this is my dear friend, Dr. Bert Moore, founder and president of PASTORCARE, The National Clergy Support Network in Raleigh, North Carolina. I just received the news, while tweaking this chapter, that Dr. Moore lost his fight with cancer and is now being cared for by the Ultimate Caregiver. This man, who was abandoned by his wife and made it through a horrendous divorce, turned that which was meant by the enemy to destroy him into an incredible ministry of "helps" to others.

There is even an annual conference called the CareGivers Forum (www.caregiversforum.org), a yearly gathering of people from across the United States and elsewhere who are involved in the ministry of caring for professional Christian workers and their families. They provide an annual forum for personal relationships, professional networking and shared learning opportunities.

The Forum began in 1989 as a venue for ministry leaders to gather and share their concerns and visions. Over the years it has evolved into a network of like-minded people concerned about supporting each other in the sometimes difficult task of "ministering to ministers."

Forum attendees come from a variety of ministry settings: from places providing leisure and recreation retreats, to places providing comprehensive mental health services (and everything in between).

Everyone is welcome: from the individual who is contemplating starting a new ministry, to leaders of well-established ministries.

The Forum is guided by a steering committee of volunteers which seeks to provide a balanced environment of small group interaction, larger, group input, and ample free time to network, problem solve and grow spiritually.

Another great resource (of which Encouragement Dynamics is a part) is the *Pastoral Ministries* division of Focus on the Family. They publish a pastoral directory each year, available in hard copy or online. This great resource list will guide you to care-giving ministries specializing in the needs and issues of pastoral families.

What are some specific things that you can do for your pastor and his family? Pray for them. The greatest gift you can give your pastor is to take the time to pray for him. We need to realize that pastors and other ministers are prime targets for the Devil. If he can cause a believer to fall, it's a victory for his kingdom. But, if he can cause a minister to fall, he can hurt the lives of many other believers. We have a responsibility before God to hold up our leaders in prayer, and seek God's protection over their lives.

Be reasonable in your expectations. Too many

people expect the pastor to do (and be) everything. I have heard stories about people expecting their pastor to pick up their children from school, talk to them when they can't sleep, mow their lawn, and fix their car. God has given specific instructions regarding what your pastor is to do and who he is to be. You are to do everything in your power to protect him, so that he can fulfill the call and anointing God has placed upon his life.

Compensate him appropriately. There's an old joke about a church board praying something like this, "Lord, you keep our pastor humble, and we'll keep him poor." That attitude is far too common. Pastors and their families have the same financial needs as everyone else in the congregation. In fact, they often have more expenses, because of the needs of visiting people and costs incurred as they minister to them.

When I go into a church, I always try to get with the leaders of the church to discuss some things that the pastor will never discuss. I tell pastors, "You need me to come to your church to tell your men what you would like them to know but you will never tell them." The obvious reason for this is because it will sound "self-serving" if it comes from the pastor. It is during this meeting that I discuss the proper salary and compensation package for the pastor.

I remember when I was going through the candidate process at a certain church. The topic of the pastor's salary came up. One of the men said, "I believe we should pay the pastor an average of what the people in the church make." I immediately told the group, "If you are looking for an average pastor then you do not want me for your pastor. I'm not an average pastor." I believe a good guideline for us to use today in compensating a pastor is that he should receive slightly more than the average income of his congregation. He should also receive a car allowance, gasoline allowance, expenses for entertainment to be used for the congregation, an education allowance for him to pursue higher education, etc. This will allow his family to live and minister without having to worry about money.

Respect his privacy and time. Often being a pastor is a 24-hour a day job. Granted, there are always emergencies that come up at the most inopportune times. But a hangnail or the flu is not an emergency. Your pastor needs time to study, time to pray, time to rest and time to be with *his* family.

One of my pet peeves is the treatment of pastors' children. Pastors' children have become a joke in our society today. Although the church expects them to be perfect, the world expects them to be hellions. Why? Because they usually are! Why? Because Dad is so busy taking care of everyone else, he does not have time for his own family. Do not expect him to give up his wife and children to take care of yours. That's your job.

Let your pastor and his wife know you appreciate them. Everyone needs some encouragement now and then. One of the motivational gifts mentioned in Romans 12:6-8 is exhortation and encouragement. This gift is badly lacking in the Body of Christ today. It is especially lacking toward those in ministry. We expect them to encourage us, forgetting that they need it as well. A kind or encouraging word, a card, or even a small gift will work wonders to build up your pastor and help him continue in the calling God has given him.

When I'm speaking at a church, at the end of my message I ask the pastor, his wife and his family to come forward so I can say a special prayer for them. I make two comments and, when I do, I can literally see the mouths of the congregation fall open. The first comment is: "Have you ever thought about the fact that there is one man in this church who does not have a pastor? That is this man here. The second is: Has it ever occurred to you that there is one lady in the church who shares her husband with everyone else in the church and that is this lady here?"

It never fails that, at the end of the service, people in the congregation come up to me and thank me. The usual comment is: "Thank you Dr. Pinion. What you said never occurred to me before, and I promise to encourage my pastor and his wife more."

Chapter 7

RESTRUCTURE

Understanding Essence and Roles.

Prepare to feel obsolete. It's the first step to moving ahead.
—Elizabeth Weil

I believe that the one problem underlying all others is that we have been sold a traditional "bill of goods," and we have moved both pastors and churches from a community model led by a shepherd to a corporation model run by a CEO. This type of structure is designed for control instead of growth. It promotes division and disunity instead of harmony and unity. And the very promoter of all of it is an infrastructure where the sheep are controlling and leading the shepherd!

We have chosen standardization over uniqueness. We have chosen predictability over surprise. And, without realizing it, to our own regret, we have chosen comfort and convenience over servanthood and sacrifice.

In the end, what we have chosen is organization over life; and this, perhaps, is the fundamental dilemma we face—that, at best, the church is seen as a healthy institution.

The church is seen as the religious equivalent of IBM or Microsoft. If the church is not running well, the solutions clearly lie in the best business practices available. Do not get me wrong here. I'm not by any means suggesting that we do not use "business principles." But when we choose to operate via business principles instead of Biblical principles, it sets the stage for the pastor to be the CEO. The success of the church, *if* it occurs, then rests in its ability to move from a "mom and pop" business to a conglomerate corporation. *Robert's Rules of Order then* becomes the guiding principle rather that the pattern of the New Testament church, and again setting the stage for the sheep to control the shepherd.

Is it any wonder that 80 percent of seminary and Bible school graduates who enter the ministry will leave the ministry within the first five years![1] Can you imagine how frustrating this can be to someone just out of seminary who believes with all his heart that God has called him to enter the ministry? While he may have tasted only a little of what that means, *pastor* is the image that filled his original vision. But when he gets to his first church, it's nothing like what he saw in his call. It certainly is not what his professors (who have not pastored at all or have not pastored in many years) told him church life would be like. Now his leading sheep tell him that he must come up with a six-year strategic plan. He must also create and manage the budget. And, "Oh, by the way, here is our list of twenty things that the CEO does at this church and, by the way, we don't like change!" All the while, the new pastor is thinking, "But I'm here because I care about people." So, while he is trying to fulfill the CEO expectations forced upon him by the controlling sheep, he figures that if he can get another one hundred people to attend his church, he will feel better about ministry. So the Lord blesses and another hundred people come.

Honeymoon over! Now it's just a matter of time until that frazzled pastor gets tired of beating his head against the wall and throws in the proverbial towel. Or, in the case of many shepherds, they become so weary and worn out from the controls placed on them and the cruel battle of "high expectations" that they give up and are run out of the church by the controlling sheep.

God's chosen and called shepherds know instinctively that success is not measured by fulfilling the corporation's expectations. Pastors I deal with make comments like, "I really thought I could be used of

God to build a strong and viable work here. If it had not been for a few people, we could have built a great church." That's a major reason why pastors change churches, on average, every eighteen months.[2] In nearly every case where I have dealt with a wounded, hurt and discouraged pastor, I have noticed that the wounds were not caused from *responsibilities* but *resistance*!

One pastor friend of mine recently wrote me the following:

> Five years ago I went through some incredible pain at my church when some of the old control guards decided they would start having secret meetings and call for my dismissal. My enemies, about 10 percent of a growing, thriving congregation that had tripled in the 13 years while I was their pastor, finally got to me and I resigned in discouragement, pain, and grief. People who I thought would stand up for me didn't, and I felt betrayed. As I reflect, I don't know too many pastors who have not experienced this pain to one extent or another.

Yes, my friend, we *have* all, at one time or another "experienced this pain to one extent or another." It's *this* type of pain that has been the proverbial "nail in the coffin," or the aneurysm that abruptly ended the divine calling of many pastors. Mark Twain once said, "If a cat sits on a hot stove, that cat won't sit on a hot stove again. That cat won't sit on a cold stove either. In fact, that cat won't sit on stoves period!" Pastors can sometimes feel like the cat on the church's stove.

Most pastors cherish and love the calling, but the tangential bureaucracy of modern church life is driving them crazy: the spats over bulletins; the arguing over the color of the choir robes; the quarrels over the music; the bickering about the times of the services; the disagreeing over what clothes should or shouldn't be worn in the services; the "paralysis of analysis" that goes on in the board meetings; the complaining about the length, or lack of length, of the sermons. I even had a lady in one of the churches I pastored leave the church because someone was sitting in *her* pew! No wonder pastors lie in their beds on Sunday mornings debating whether to get up or hide under the mattress! Interestingly, most church members go through the same thing.

God is not the author of confusion! ". . . God doesn't stir us up into confusion; he brings us into harmony" (I Corinthians 14:33 MSG). "But let all things be done decently and in order" (I Corinthians 14:40 NIV). One of the reasons many pastors, church leaders and members deal with so much unnecessary conflict, confusion, discord, dissension and disharmony is because they do not have a clear understanding of "essence" and "roles."

There is a divine design and nothing functions outside this realm. Whether it is a church, a family or even the Trinity, there can be no function without implementation of this divine design!

Let me explain. *Essence* is the quality or qualities of a thing that give it its identity: the indispensable properties of a thing. *Roles,* on the other hand, are the characteristics and expected social behaviors of an individual, a function or a position.

Let's take the family. We have the husband (father), the wife (mother) and the children. In essence, they are all the same. "You are all sons of God through faith in Christ Jesus, for all of you who were baptized into Christ have clothed yourselves with Christ. There is neither Jew nor Greek, slave nor free, male nor female, for you are all one in Christ Jesus" (Galatians 3:26-28 NKJV). Remember *essence*—all the same!

However, in *roles* there is a huge difference. So, just as the church submits to Christ as He exercises such leadership, wives should likewise submit to their husbands. "Husbands, go all out in your love for your wives, exactly as Christ did for the church—a love marked by giving, not getting. Christ's love makes the church whole. His words evoke her beauty. Everything He does and says is designed to bring the best out of her, dressing her in dazzling white silk, radiant with holiness. And that is how husbands ought to love their wives. They're really doing themselves a favor—since they're already *one* in marriage. No one abuses his own body, does he? No, he feeds and pampers it. That's how Christ treats us, the church, since we are part of His body. And this is why a man leaves father and mother and cherishes his wife. No longer two, they become *one flesh*. This is a huge mystery, and I don't pretend to understand it all. What is clearest to me is the way Christ treats the church. And this provides a good picture of how each husband is to treat his wife, loving himself in loving her, and how each wife is to honor her husband. Children, do what your parents tell you. This is only right. 'Honor your father and mother' is the first commandment that has a promise attached to it, namely, 'so you will live well and have a long life'" (Ephesians 5:25-6:3 MSG). No order, no function!

How about the Trinity? We have God the Father, Jesus Christ, and the Holy Spirit. In *essence*, all the same; in *roles*, they are uniquely different. No order, no function.

Let's carry this same analogy over to the church. We have the pastor, the lay leaders and the congregation. In *essence,* there is no difference. But in *roles,* there is a huge difference. The pastor (even though he is a sheep) is the shepherd; the lay leaders and the congregation are the sheep. When the shepherd does not take on his divine role, there is no function. Likewise, when the sheep try to *control* the shepherd, there is *no* function!

That's why this Biblical structure must be implemented, taught and adhered to. Otherwise we have total chaos, confusion and no function!

It is not my intent to do an exhaustive study on the polity or governance of the local church. However, after years of neglect, church polity has once again become the topic of discussion in many circles of faith. This is occurring in churches, seminaries and Bible colleges and among church leaders. This recent resurgence of interest in church polity has been fueled by the concern of many in conforming and/or returning to a more Biblical form of church governance. Many are questioning whether they have been practicing the right method of church structure/governance (particularly with regard to pastoral, deacon and congregational authority).

How did we get in this mess? Beginning early in the second century, many religious leaders and churches abandoned the Biblically-mandated model and basis for church leadership consisting of two offices (elders and deacons). they adopted a new model: three offices within each local church consisting of one bishop, a council of elders and a body of deacons.

In time, this tradition based system moved further and further away from the Biblical model established in the New Testament. This tradition became the initial basis for episcopatory—structured churches such as the Roman Catholic Church, the Church of England and the Episcopal Church.

Just as ultimate political power can corrupt, so too religious power can corrupt; historically, that is exactly what happened. Alexander Strauch has outlined this process in his book, *Biblical Eldership,* as follows: "At the start of the second century, the overseer (bishop) presided over one local church, not a group of churches; thus, he is called the monarchical bishop. Through the centuries, inordinate authority became concentrated in the bishop." Strauch goes on to say, "Unchecked by the New Testament Scriptures, his role continued to expand. The bishop became ruler over a group of churches. Some bishops emerged as supreme over other bishops. Eventually they formed councils of bishops."

Alexander Strauch concludes by stating, "Finally, in the West, one bishop emerged as head over every Christian and every church."

But in the churches of the New Testament period, there was no clearly defined, three-office system. Instead, there were only two offices, as found in Philippians 1:1.

The tradition of man established titles, roles and offices, such as pope, cardinal, archbishop, bishop, monsignor, right reverend and reverend. The early Christians were consistently referred to as brother, sister, slave, bond slave, servant, steward, soldier, prisoner, beloved and the like. While the Romans, Greeks and religious Jews were impressed with titles, the New Testament declares that all true Christians are *saints* by calling (I Corinthians 1:2) and *priests* by the new birth of all those purchased by the blood of Jesus Christ (I Peter 1:18-19, 2:5,9).

The tradition of man produced titles. The New Testament Christians produced testimonies!

It has been my experience that many of the conflicts that divide, split, splinter and kill pastors *and* churches are usually over the issue of control. When the right and Biblical structure/governance/polity is in place, and we understand and implement essence and roles, we will then see harmony, unity and health as God intends.

Chapter 8

REINVENT

Unlearning church.

Think of life today as being lived in the "pressure tense"
(present + future) because that's what it is,
and that's where you are.
—Watts Wacker and Jim Taylor

The other day I came across a cartoon portraying two pastors having coffee at a neighborhood cafe. The caption below the cartoon read, "We're in debt, the deacons have all quit and we've not had a visitor in six months. But thank goodness none of the other churches are doing any better!" As humorous as this may sound, it could be the true conversation on the lips of thousands of frustrated pastors across America today.

I personally believe that, when the horse dies, it's time to dismount! As a pastor, I have always felt that if a particular ministry has lost its efficiency and effectiveness, then it's time to "let it die." Usually when something is dead, it begins to stink; and when it stinks, its time to bury it!

I remember receiving a phone call from a pastor in the Midwest. He was weeping uncontrollably as he shared with me that, in the past ten years, he has taken his church from a weekly attendance of over 700 to less than 200. He said, "I'm merely treading water to stay a float."

Another pastor wrote to me with these words, "I have been discouraged, dismayed and disenchanted many times, but never experienced the feeling of being dysfunctional as I have in the past five or six years."

Another pastor I recently had breakfast with is the senior pastor of one of the greatest and most effective churches in America today. With tears streaming down his cheeks he said, "I told my wife that I am about ready to resign my church, leave the ministry, and get a 9 to 5 job at Wal-Mart."

While writing this book, hunkered in a cabin like a hermit in the mountains in northern Idaho (by now I'm sort of feeling like Grizzly Adams), I took a break and journeyed into Boise one morning to have breakfast with a church planter and dear friend of mine.

Both my friend and I were cut out of the same denominational (whoops—we're not supposed to use the *denominational* word); I mean, *fellowship*, church mold. He asked me, "What would you do if you were planting a church in today's world?" This question was in the context of our previous discussion, reminiscing about the "good ol' days."

We both came to the conclusion and realization that we were getting older and didn't have much time left to do what God had called us to do, so there was no room for any mistakes. We realized that we were faced with the urgency to do church right and had both experienced diminishing returns on our investment of money, time and energy. Like other church leaders of the past five decades, we were trying to figure out how to do church better.

During our ministries, we had jumped through all the church growth hoops: utilizing ministry products such as consultants, seminars, parachurch ministries, publishing houses, etc., that pawned their shelves of methodological books, prodding us to push the church toward the next current fad.

Our conversation continued to encapsulate the current church growth methods: offer small groups, have a contemporary service, create a spiritual experience, become seeker-friendly, create an environment of high-expectation member culture, make sure we purify the church from bad doctrine, be relational, and, last but not least, let's not forget to be "purpose driven."

There is nothing inherently wrong with any of these methods, but they do make me, and other church leaders I have talked with, a little skeptical about the next new, guaranteed method that will come along and tell us how to build a perfect church.

My advice to my friend was, "Realize that nothing is more important than you listening to God and passionately portraying and communicating the vision and direction that He has given to you to reach your city and your world. Don't be afraid to step out by faith; take risks and don't be afraid of change. If there was ever a time for on-the-edge, over-the-top, out-of-the-box leadership, it is now!"

I couldn't help remembering a class I had in graduate school: *The Pastor and Leadership*. Our adjunct professor was Leith Anderson, pastor of Wooddale Church (in the Minneapolis suburb of Eden Prairie, Minnesota), who authored the great books, *A Church for the 21st Century*, *Dying for Change*, and *Winning the Values War in a Changing Culture*. The discussion centered on all the so-called trends that were prevalent during the early 90s that offered certain sure-to-work methods for building a church. After discussing many of these trends, I remember raising my hand. With tears flowing down my cheeks, I made this statement: "It seems to me like I'm earnestly, diligently and painfully trying to figure out how to unlock the lock; and, about the time I find the right key, someone changes the lock!"

This brings me to the point where I must talk about a word considered so dirty in many of our churches today that it conjures up almost immediate hostility, resentment and opposition. A word that, when uttered, has cost many a pastor his job and has been the catalyst of banishment for others in the ministry. A word so feared that, if it must be used, is couched in euphemisms or coded church ghetto language. The word is *change*!

George Barna once said this about the resistance to change: "One of the most prevalent obstacles to renewal is people's resistance to change." Study after study in the secular marketplace has demonstrated that the organizations that leapfrog ahead of the competition are those that lead their key audiences (executives, employees, shareholders and consumers) to be at peace with the necessity for, and process of, change. The acceptance of new ways for new outcomes is critical to a church comeback.

You have probably experienced the amazing capacity of people to avoid change in their personal environment. If our churches showed half the creativity in winning the world for Christ that they exhibit in their resistance to new ministry ideas, real revival would take place.

The resistance movement may start with the familiar, "but we've never done it that way." The battle escalates from there, with the excuses becoming more and more creative. People who have remained in the shadows for years suddenly become prescient, able to anticipate looming barriers and problems that others simply are not "gifted" to perceive. Invariably, as the new pastor moves to make his mark on the ministry and begins to reverse the downward spiral of the church, murmurs are heard that "the pastor is moving too fast."

Carl F. George, in *Prepare Your Church for the Future*, talks about how, as a youngster, he grew up near a small mom-and-pop store. Reminiscing, he says:

> Pop typically hovered around the hardware section, tinkering with fasteners he sold for two cents apiece, but that, considering overhead costs, should have sold for twenty-five cents. Pop liked his puttering because he could get to know the customers. His relationship building helped patrons feel good about their visit, and it ensured that they'd come again.
>
> Mom focused her energies in the well-organized housewives' department. By featuring attractive, fashionable items, her profits

more than compensated for the money lost on the under-priced fasteners.

Mom and Pop lacked the business vocabulary to articulate ideas like: pinpointing their center of growth (housewares), capitalizing on their strengths (Pop's problem solving ability and Mom's eye for newer lines), and reinforcing the reasons they initially opened the store (serving customers and maximizing profits so as to support the family).

To Mom and Pop, running the store had become a way of life. The daily rituals—sweeping the sidewalk and straightening the merchandise— provided them a sense of security and comfort.

One day Mom and Pop realized that the needs of their customers had been changing. Lately, some had indicated that getting in and out of a store quickly was more important than chatting with the proprietor. Others didn't want to buy merchandise unless they could choose from at least three different brands. As a result, the people Mom and Pop wanted to serve were going elsewhere.

Mom and Pop sensed this dissonance and interpreted it as an ultimatum for change. They decided to survive; Pop would install self-service hardware and Mom would take special orders. They once again placed higher priority on meeting customers' needs and maximizing profits than on maintaining the way of life they'd known and cherished.

In making these choices, Mom and Pop demonstrated how an organization can refocus its sights on the original impetus for its success. Recapturing that purpose is worth interrupting familiar routines!

Churches are faced with a similar dilemma. We quickly forget that the felt needs of our "customers" are in a constant state of flux. We can't overlook the fact that each new day ushers in a slightly different set of circumstances. We sometimes ignore the long-range implications of not keeping abreast with the present. Instead, we often persist in the comfortable habits to which we've grown accustomed.

What does our lifestyle say about our openness to change? Are we willing to face the reality that people, even spiritually hungry individuals, are passing us by as they walk down the street of life? Are we inclined to ask *why*, knowing that our blind spots might figure into the explanation?

We need to take a fresh look at what God has called us to be. We need a way of measuring our health and effectiveness. And we need a readiness to generate changes that are needed.

I believe the choices that challenge Christians today are so great that many local churches' very existence is, or will soon be, at stake.

Fortunately, many men and women in leadership aren't ignoring the future. Evangelical researchers are pinpointing significant trends of the 1990s and are discovering new Biblical models that God can use to seize the opportunities of our day. Churches are acknowledging that, for our own spiritual health, much less survival, we must change.[1]

Lyle E. Schaller, in his book, *Strategies for Change*, says:

From a different perspective, another question can be asked. What is the number-one issue facing Christian organizations on the North American continent today? What is the one issue that faces every congregation, denomination, movement, theological seminary, parachurch organization and inter church agency? Dwindling numbers? Money? Social justice? Competent leadership? The growing dysfunctional nature of ecclesiastical structures? Television? The new immigration from the Pacific Rim and Latin America? Governmental regulations? Human sexuality? The fact our society has become an increasingly barren and hostile environment for rearing children? The shift from verbal to visual communication?

After more than three decades spent working with thousands of congregational, denominational, seminary and parachurch leaders from more than five dozen traditions, this observer places one issue at the top of that list: "the need to initiate and implement planned change from within an organization." That is the number-one issue today facing most congregations, denominations, theological seminaries, parachurch organizations and reform movements.

One subject will illustrate that statement. During the past three decades, tens of millions of words have been published on church growth. Several denominations have made church growth a high priority.

The Church Growth Movement has produced a huge variety of valuable insights and resources for those interested in promoting numerical growth. Opponents of that movement have marshaled arguments to explain why this emphasis on numerical growth falls somewhere between heretical and demonic.

The neglected facet of this debate is that numerical growth is not the issue, but rather a product of a larger concern.

The big issue is change. The central issue in any effective strategy for numerical growth—whether by a congregation, a denomination, a theological seminary or a parachurch organization—is change. Reversing a period of numerical decline requires changes. Numerical growth also produces change."[2]

The signs we need to perceive are not vague predictions about the future—many are present realities. The trouble is that they occur so gradually that we often do not notice them. It is like the familiar story of the frog and the kettle of water. Place a frog in boiling water and it will jump out immediately because it can tell that it is in a hostile environment. However, if you place a frog in a kettle of room-temperature water, it will not leap out; it will just stay there, unaware that the environment is changing. Continue to turn up the burner until the water is boiling, and our poor frog will be boiled. He might be quite content, but he will nevertheless be dead. If we continue to do "business as usual" in our local churches, then we will continue to see our churches decline.

It will be increasingly difficult to convince the unchurched that our faith is pertinent to the 21st century if the tools of our trade are from the last century.[3] This is why, as leaders, we *must* keep relevant and up-to-date with the changes that are occurring in our society.

Many of our churches today are still trying to

operate on models of ministry that were developed several hundred years ago, ignoring the fact that the society for which that model was designed no longer exists.[4] Many in leadership positions have taken the posture that we would rather "fight than switch." This enormous allegiance to remain the same and continue to do ministry "the way we've always done it" will ultimately either kill us or add to our existing ineffectiveness in reaching our communities with the Gospel of Christ.

Albert Einstein said: "Insanity is doing the same old things—the same old way—and expecting different results."

This "traditional" posture seems to almost anesthetize our abilities to be effective in reaching and ministering to our generation. It's almost as though some churches are so "heavenly" minded that they are no "earthly" good!

Jack W. Hayford once said, "To target today's lost souls, we had better tune in to both the Holy Spirit and the realities of our culture. Focusing on one to the exclusion of the other will fail to penetrate the present with eternity's power, values and blessing."[5]

As authors Dr. William Crabb and Jeff Jernigan say in their book, *The Church in Ruins*, "A widening gap between the world views and social realities of the North American church and society is making it harder and harder for the church to reach the lost, and to meaningfully serve the saved. Fortunately, the hope for the future of the church lies in the roots of its past. But those roots cannot be grasped without a radical change of approach to ministry." Once again, the purpose of this book is to give hope and direction to those who are serious about revitalization.

It is very difficult to throw in the towel and give up the fight when there are some aggressive fellow competitors that are winning the battle.

It is imperative that we as leaders understand that many of the old approaches and traditional strategies for sharing our faith, which worked for us in the past decades, will no longer work today. We have to be clever enough to analyze our environment and provide creative responses to the challenges we now face.

Make no mistake about it; the pressures on the pastor as a leader are mounting. Typically, we have been five to ten years behind society, responding to changing conditions long after transitions have begun. We have now run out of time. If we want the Christian faith to remain a vibrant alternative to the world system, we must stop *reacting* and start *anticipating*.[6]

Elmer Towns, in his book, *Ten of Today's Most Innovative Churches*, says, "Our culture is like a drag racer, rushing toward the future. But will the church be left behind? Too many congregations are hibernating churches, withdrawing from the world, refusing to meet the challenge of society. When the kids walk into their services they groan, 'This is history.' Many churches are not keeping up, but falling behind. To listen to their pastors, they don't want to keep up. They want to hibernate until the rapture."[7]

I feel that Scripture suggests that our worship should be sensitive to the non-churched or non-Christian person. In I Corinthians 14:23-25, Paul reprimands the Corinthians for handling their worship service in such a manner that would offend non-believers. He encouraged them, instead, to worship in a way that would exalt God *and* reach people. In other words, Paul instructed them to be mindful of the way their services would impact the non-believer in attendance.

I'm certainly not against being "seeker sensitive," but not at the expense of being "Holy Spirit insensitive."

I think it would be appropriate here to remind the reader that when we talk about *change*, we are not talking about *the message*, but *the methods*. Growing churches are not tied to old programs that no longer work. They are not afraid to change! They are flexible in method, though not with the Gospel message. John Maxwell, who was one of our professors during *The Pastor and Evangelism/Church Growth* class at the

Northwest Graduate School of Ministry said, "Growth equals change, because you cannot grow unless you change. Change is the price we pay for growth."

Hippocrates, in his Aphorisms II, says, ". . .a change must sometimes be made to things one is not accustomed to."

This decade is a pivotal time in the history of churches in America. It will be a time in which the Church will either explode with new growth or quietly fade into a colorless thread in the fabric of a secular culture.

As a church, we must prove ourselves to be real and viable, or become just another spiritual philosophy bookmarked in the history of mankind. As leaders, we must develop intelligent and effective responses in service to Christ. As George Barna is careful to point out, "It will be increasingly difficult to convince the unchurched that our faith is pertinent to the 21st century if the tools of our trade are from the last century."

Robert E. Logan sums it up in his book, *Beyond Church Growth: Action Plans for Developing a Dynamic Church*, when he says, "An amazing phenomenon in the twentieth-century church is that we are still stuck in forms of worship and ministry which are more culturally appropriate to the nineteenth century. The robes, the pipe organ, the hymnals, the order of worship, and the nature and place of the sermon are all vestiges of nineteenth-century culture."

The late John F. Kennedy, in his Inaugural Address, January 20, 1961, said, "All this (speaking of space exploration) will not be finished in the first one hundred days. Nor will it be finished in the first one thousand days, nor in the life of this administration, not even perhaps in our lifetime on this planet. But let us begin."

Chapter 9

REVITALIZE

We have to do *what?*

I couldn't wait for success, so I just went ahead without it.
—Jonathan Winters

It is very difficult for me to visit a church service without putting on my *consultant* hat. This, by the way, drives my wife crazy! When I pull into the parking lot, I can usually tell whether the church is passionate about their vision. Does the landscaping look like it's been left up to God? Am I greeted when I enter? Or, could I literally walk off with the piano while nobody noticed? Are the announcements more important than the message? Is the "worship" (or lack of worship) interrupted by a staff member begging, badgering, cajoling, and/or guilting people into being volunteers?

John Bisagno, former pastor of Houston's First Baptist Church, tells the story of coming to Houston to

candidate for the position of pastor many years ago.
He said, "As I entered the auditorium, it was dimly lit,
with just a few people huddled together. They were
singing some old, slow, funeral-type song that was
depressing."

Later that day, he took a walk in downtown
Houston and came upon a jewelry store. It was some
sort of grand opening, and there were bright lights
and a greeter at the door welcoming customers with a
smile. Inside there was a celebration going on. There
were refreshments and people having a good time
talking and laughing with each other. They welcomed him and offered him some punch.

He said that, "After attending both the church and
the jewelry store, if the jewelry store had offered an
invitation, I would have joined the jewelry store."

Sometimes an organization is mentally and emotionally prepared for change, but is not ready struc-
turally. Evaluate how decisions are made, how
processes are managed, and how changes can be introduced into your church's ministry. Consider how a
larger body relying upon your church for the existing
menu of ministry services will be impacted by the
structure you have in place.

In some churches, growth is inhibited by the existing leadership structures. It might be the fact that
decisions are made by committees, or that there are

too many committees, or that the committees simply do not function adequately. Perhaps the problem is the manner in which leaders are chosen within the system, or it could be identity (or tenure) of those leaders. Or, it might be the nature of the relationship between the staff and laity, and the means of communication that exist.

Take the time to think through what kinds of leaders you will need to affect change in your church. Decide how you can get the right people in the right positions, and get them cleared to make the kinds of decisions, in a timely manner, required for progress. Start early in the growth process, before the actual acquisition efforts begin, to facilitate the kind of organizational structure that will enable a smooth process later.

Think about the logistics of how you do ministry. What times are the services and classes held? Are there alternative services? Do those times and places meet the needs of your target audience? If you can pinpoint weaknesses, then the earlier you can start preparing the congregation for changes in the ministry, the better.

What about your church policies? Do they inhibit visitors from feeling welcomed and integrated into the flow of your ministry? Do those policies enhance growth or prevent it? Realize that no policy is sacred. Many of today's most successful businesses remain profitable partially because they re-examine their infrastructure every three to five years, and reshape their company according to the current needs of their people and the prevailing environment. Be aware that clinging to tradition often limits growth. Following a pattern of activity for which you know no alternatives can be similarly stifling. Be seriously willing to study and alter every aspect of your organizational structure and policy-setting system. Recognize that your church is an organic entity; a change in one element of the entity will impact all other elements. While anticipatory change can be healthy, also remember that change for its own sake can be devastating.

Reggie McNeal tells a story about visiting a church in part of the state that was unfamiliar to him. He said, "The church had no sign on the road or even on the church property. The only clue I had that I was at the right place was a church van in the parking lot with the church's name on it. Before I got out of my car, I knew the congregation was not expecting any non-club members to show up. Sure enough, what I discovered inside was a group of people content to grow older and fewer in number as long as they could enjoy their religious club meetings and keep member services paid for (including the chaplain 'pastor' they hired to look after them). The pastor told me that new people to the area didn't feel welcome there. I never would have known!"

He then tells of an experience contrasting the above story. He said, "A pastor friend of mine pastors a congregation whose member and ministry efforts are fueled by a vision to be missionaries to their community. Everything from the artistry of the banners in the worship center to the fresh smell in the rest rooms screams that someone is paying attention. Every week scores of volunteers show up early to set up tables, put out literature, set up chairs, go through sound checks and perform dozens of other tasks. These folks do it cheerfully, willingly and enthusiastically. Their energy is palpable. Their commitment and excellence reflect the fact that they have been captured by a vision of community transformation, and they are eager to make their personal contribution to the effort."[1]

One report on church growth estimated that pastor tenure was directly related to church health and growth. In the samples employed, 73 percent of the growing churches had a pastor with tenure of four or more years, as compared to only 35 percent of declining churches. One of the more obvious reasons that many pastors swap churches so frequently is that they suffer ministry "burnout." This usually occurs when pastors become frustrated because they are totally oblivious to styles and methods of ministry, except for the traditional ways that have been handed down from leaders of decades gone by. When this happens, frustration sets in and the only way to deal with it seems to be to find greener pastures.

Many pastors leave their current churches in search of the illusive "dream church," instead of learning new and creative ways to "do church." These pastors struggle to make sense of their new environment and culture, and they fail to realize that the church has the chance to offer real, practical, Biblical solutions to our nation. When this happens, it is just a matter of time before they land back in the "burnout" phase.

When a pastor is constantly packing and unpacking luggage, spending more time writing resumes than sermons, and more time meeting with search committees than ministering to hurting members of the body, ministry is compromised. You cannot maximize your potential if you are always looking over your shoulder. Leaders in the church should allow the pastor to plant his roots and engage in a long-term pastorate: leading the church to accomplish the special vision that God has ordained for that place with him at the helm. Effective leadership can only be facilitated by a long-term commitment to a church.

How easy it is to give so much for so long, with so little time for refreshment and appreciation, that the flame of desire gets extinguished. Our society, as well as the church, offers little time for personal renewal. The focus is on progress—pushing ahead full speed at all times. Pastors who demand regular periods of recreation and solitary reflection are viewed as sluggards. The workaholic personality is subtly appreciated—until burnout hits, at which time the workaholic is castigated for ineffectual performance.

I was once accused of "playing golf too much and neglecting my *job* at the church." Fortunately, every time you play at a course you sign in, or have to have a tee time, or both. I have always made it a practice to keep all I do, and where and when I do it, on my calendar. I also made it a point to tell my executive secretary when I left the office and where I was going.

One of my leaders and board members was an FBI agent. I was tired of hearing the untrue accusations about my "playing too much golf and being out of the office so frequently," so I told the board that I would gladly turn my calendar over to Mr. FBI agent, as well as grant him permission to talk with my executive assistant to *investigate* me. After a week or so, the FBI agent called a special board meeting to give the results of his findings. He reported to the board that, "It appears that our pastor is not guilty of the charges against him. He works well over 60 hours a week and has never taken his entire vacation or all of his days off. If anything, we owe *him* time off." Just the false accusation could have been the beginnings of my downfall.

Misconceptions about pastoral responsibilities abound. According to an article that was given to me by one of my parishioners, pastors have nothing to do except:

- To decide what is to be done; to get somebody to do it; to listen to reasons why it should not be done, why it should be done by somebody else, or why it should be done a different way.

- To follow up to see if the thing has been done, only to discover that it has not; to inquire why it has not been done; and to listen to excuses from the one who was supposed to do it.

- To follow up again to see if it has yet been done, only to discover that it has been done incorrectly and to point out how it should be done. To conclude that since it has been done, it may as well be left as it is.

- To wonder if it is not time to sideline a person who cannot do what he is told to do. To reflect that this person has considerable influence

upon others in the congregation; to remember
that he is rather "thin skinned"; to conclude
that his successor will probably be as bad and
maybe worse.

• To consider how much simpler and better it
would have been to do the thing himself in the
first place; to reflect sadly that he could have
done it right in twenty minutes, but as it
turned out, he has spent two days to find out
why it has taken three weeks for someone else
to do it wrong.

The plain truth is that the shorter the period of
time a pastor has in which to operate, the less impact
he is likely to have in that ministry. Study the most
effective pastors across the nation and you will find
that, while most of them began to have a significant
impact within their first three years in the new position, they have had a steadily growing impact over the
course of their tenure, in most cases even up through
their second decade.

Chapter 10

REJOICE

It's great being back in church!

The Christian life is but a constant re-beginning, a return to grace every day, sometimes even every hour, through Him who, after each failure, pardons so that all things should be made new.
—Robert Schutz, *This Day Belongs to God*

In Bill Hybels' book, *Courageous Leadership,* he makes the following statement: "There is nothing like the local church when it's working right. Its beauty is indescribable. Its power is breathtaking. Its potential is unlimited. It comforts the grieving and heals the broken in the context of community. It builds bridges to seekers and offers truth to the confused. It provides resources for those in need and opens its arms to the forgotten, the downtrodden, and the disillusioned. It breaks the chains of addictions, frees the oppressed, and offers belonging to the marginalized of this world.

Whatever the capacity for human suffering, the church has a greater capacity for healing and wholeness. Still, to this day, the potential of the local church is almost more than I can grasp. No other organization on earth is like the church. Nothing even comes close."[1] In my opinion, there could be no greater truth!

I am, and have been for my nearly 30 years of ministry, what George Barna refers to as a "turn-around" pastor. Turn-around pastors tend to be team builders, visionaries, strategic thinkers, risk takers and encouragers. Every church I have pastored has grown numerically due to my gift as a relational evangelist. I spoke of this in the introduction of this book.

As a result of seeing new people come through the doors of the church, I always ended up having basically two congregations under one roof. Yet, I always seemed to hit a barrier around my fifth year at a church. As a result, I had to try to find a balance between ministering to the new people coming in, as well as the old guard that was there when I came.

What do I know now that I didn't know then? In the end, it is not so much about prolonging or perpetuating our own life (both the new people and the old guard), but rather about giving new life to others. The more we focus on our own living, the less we are concerned about giving life to others.

I believe with all my heart that life-giving churches don't exist for themselves; they exist for those who don't know life Himself: Christ. The reason God gives us His life is to impact our world.

Let me explain! For several years I went fishing with a dear old saint and friend (who has since gone on to be with the Lord) and his two sons on the Kenai River in Alaska. It was always an incredible experience. I learned the amazing habits of one of God's most inspiring creations: the Alaskan salmon. A salmon will swim miles and miles, working its way upstream to the place it was hatched from an egg, for the sole purpose of spawning a new generation— at the cost of her own life! Whether instinct tells a salmon that it's time to die, or that it's time to give birth even at the cost of death, I am uncertain. But I know that even nature declares that life and death are inseparable.

It is no different for the church. Jesus reminds us that unless a seed first dies, it cannot produce life. He tells us that unless we lose our own lives, we will never live. It should be no surprise to us that the church is the most productive when she is committed to giving herself away that others may live.

God created every living creature with the capacity to create life. Even the plants bear seeds. A non-reproducing species will live only one generation, but a species that reproduces—barring natural catastrophe—will live as long as time exists. Species do not have to be taught to reproduce. It is inherent in their nature. My good friend, Pastor Ken Hutcherson, raises world champion Rottweilers. He told me, "As long as I keep those dogs healthy, they will reproduce." The church must be released to do that which comes naturally.

I love the illustration Erwin McManus uses in his book, *An Unstoppable Force, Daring to Become the Church God Had In Mind.* He says, "Years ago my wife, Kim, took me to her home in the mountains of North Carolina. She grew up on a farm with her foster parents, Theodore and Ruth Davis. Theodore was walking me around the farm, and he introduced me to a mule. He went on to explain that a mule was a combination of horse and donkey. This seemed a little weird to me, so I asked him why they didn't just use a horse or a donkey. He explained that while horses are very bright in comparison to donkeys, they're not as strong. And donkeys, while they're very strong, are not bright enough to do the work necessary. When you combine the two, you get the perfect combination for the task required. But he went on to explain to me that, while mules are good for work, they cannot reproduce. Mules are best known for being stubborn and sterile."[2]

Stubborn and sterile! Sound familiar? You want a real shock? Just ask the leadership in your church (just the leaders), "When was the last time *you* led someone to Christ and when was the last time *you* brought a friend to church?"

Charles H. Spurgeon, on Sunday morning, July 18, 1858, at the Music Hall, Royal Surrey Gardens, preached the following:

> You lazy, lie-a-bed Christians, that go up to your churches and chapels and take your seats and hear our sermons and talk about getting good, but never think about doing good; ye that are letting hell fill beneath you and yet are too idle to stretch out your hands to pluck brands from the eternal burning; ye that see sin running down your streets, yet can never put so much as your foot to turn or stem the current; I wonder not that you have to complain of the littleness of your faith. It ought to be little; you do but little. And why should God give you more strength than you mean to use? Strong faith must always be an exercised faith, and he that dares not exercise the faith he has, shall not have more. "Take away from him the one talent and give it to him that hath, because he did not put it out to usury."

I suppose one of the questions a pastor is asked most is, "Pastor, how do I know God's will for my life?" Or, "How do I know God's will for my church or my ministry?" No answer will suffice. Why? We want a detailed map or plan, and we want it *now*! We want God to spell it out so we can follow the instructions. But even then, it's like me trying to put my barbecue grill together with its gazillion pieces. Sure, there is an instruction manual enclosed, but who wants to take the time and energy to read the manual?!

Too often we want God's will for us to be clear and uncomplicated, but God simply doesn't work like that. For most of us, and the people in our churches, the most spiritual thing we can do is to *do* something..."Just Do It!" Maybe we need to turn right when we want to turn left.

Many of us in ministry and in the church must move beyond simply choosing between right and wrong. We must resolve not only to leave the path of doing evil, but also to passionately pursue a life of doing good. The danger is getting stuck between the two: living in the neutral zone—where there is no real evil to speak about, but no great good to be proud of either. This will take us on a path where, instead of having nothing to be ashamed of, we will be ashamed of doing nothing. I believe God sees our life as a *tragedy* when we choose to passively watch life rather than live it. We choose to endure life instead of enjoying life!

Jesus described as wicked the person who leaves his talent unused. When we fail to choose, we choose to fail. You cannot put your life, your ministry, or your church on hold! Have you ever done nothing about a toothache in hopes it would just go away? Choosing not to choose does not put off the problem; it only exacerbates it.

God has designed our lives, our ministry and our church to move through time with intentionality. Remember the quote by Reggie McNeal I used in the introduction? In his book *The Present Future, Six Tough Questions for the Church*, he says, "[The church] lacks spiritual purpose and missional vitality. When you become a part of God's movement, you *are* a missionary. Every missionary has a mission. The mission gives him both intentionality and purpose. He has no minutes to waste. He is required to seize every divine moment."

Erwin McManus hits the nail square on the head in his book, *Dare to Live a Life of Adventure, Seizing Your Divine Moment*. He writes, "When someone near us seizes his divine moment, it stirs something within us. A lifetime of passivity only makes dormant our longing for adventure. A life where endless moments are left buried in the cemetery of unfulfilled opportunities may grow cold, but not dead. Until our bodies return to dust, there will always be a voice crying out within us to move from existence to life. The possibilities that await us in each moment are fueled by the potential God has placed within us. Seizing your divine moment is not simply about opportunity; at the core, it is about essence. It's about the kind of life you live as a result of the person you are becoming. The challenges you are willing to face will rise in proportion to the character you are willing to develop. With depth of Godly character comes an intensity of Godly passion. It is in this process of transformation that we find the fuel to engage with confidence the opportunities placed before us."

He then says something that should have a profound impact on you. I know it had a profound impact on me. "For some strange reason, many believers have come to think that their passions are always in conflict with God's purpose. Yet the psalmist said, 'Delight yourself in the Lord and he will give you the desires of your heart' (Psalm 37:4). When you draw near to God, God infuses passion, God works through human desires. To have no desires is to be without passion. A person who lives without passion is someone who is literally apathetic. When we delight in God, we become anything but apathetic. In fact, we become intensely passionate. These desires of our hearts are born out of the heart of God. The more you love God, the more deeply you care about life. The more deeply you care about people, the more deeply you are committed to making a difference in people's lives."[3]

It's time for the church to pursue something else. The executive leader (CEO) model, where the sheep control the shepherd, has to go. God's model is servant/shepherds serving under the Great Shepherd with the sheep following. This model was demonstrated by His Son, taught to His disciples, and prophesied to future Israel: "Then I will give you shepherds after my own heart, who will lead you with knowledge and understanding" (Jeremiah 3:15). Paul explained all this to the church at Corinth, whose members were debating who had the best pastor, the most effective speaker, the greatest leader, and so on. Paul recognized this posturing as an indication of life lived in "the flesh": a life outside of the power of God, that boasts in itself rather than in Him.

A Lesson from the Geese

As each goose flaps its wings, it creates uplift for the bird immediately following. By flying in a V formation, the whole flock adds at least 71 percent greater flying range than if each bird flew on its own. We can certainly learn a lesson from this illustration from

God's remarkable creation. Christians who share a common direction and a sense of community can reach their objective quicker and easier, because they are traveling on the thrust of one another.

Also, whenever a goose falls out of formation, it suddenly feels the drag and resistance of trying to go it alone, and quickly gets back into formation to take advantage of the lifting power of the bird immediately in front. If we had as much sense as a goose, we would stay in formation with those who are headed the same way we are going.

When the lead goose gets tired, he rotates back in the wing and another goose flies point. It pays to take turns doing hard jobs—with people at church or with geese flying south.

Also, the geese honk from behind to encourage those up front to keep up their speed.

Finally, when a goose gets sick, or is wounded by a shot and falls out, two geese fall out of formation and follow him down to help and protect him. They stay with him until he is either able to fly, or until he is dead. They then launch out on their own to find another formation or to catch up with their original group.

We, too, need to stand by one another; be a windbreak in someone's life—a true encourager. By ourselves, we are weak and fragile; but together, with the Lord's strength, we can encourage one another.

A story has circulated about Vince Lombardi's last season as head coach of the Green Bay Packers. Certainly those who worked for and around him knew the game of football. But on this day, he faced a difficult challenge: where to begin after yesterday's humiliating defeat. There was little he could say to his team that hadn't already been said. There were few aspects of the game that they had not agonized over and analyzed extensively. These men were professionals. They knew that their performance on the field yesterday had been atrocious. They knew their performance bore no resemblance to their game plan. They were angry, frustrated and disappointed, to say the least.

In his remarkable, deliberate manner, Lombardi met the challenge head-on. Picking up the familiar oblong, leather ball, he went directly to the heart of the matter. He brought everyone's attention back to the basics with five simple words: "Men, this is a football." One of his players who understood exactly how badly they needed to review the essentials spoke up, "Hold on Coach, you're going too fast!"

The challenge before us is similar to that of Lombardi's. In the church today there are few matters we haven't studied and discussed extensively. There is little to be said that will not sound familiar. And yet, there is much room for us to grow in our effectiveness at carrying on the mission of Christ.

Just as Lombardi began that day by forcing his men to look at the fundamentals of the game, we need to begin by holding up our "football." We need to ask the question, "What is God's plan for the church to reach our world for the cause of Christ?"

I'm an avid golfer. A good day on the course can be beautiful and enjoyable, even great fun. But on a bad day, it can be one of the most humbling and frustrating experiences you ever willfully inflict upon yourself. A cup in my office says it best, "Golf is a beautiful walk spoiled by a small white ball." There you are: a capable adult staring down at a tiny white ball. In your hand you hold a fairly simple instrument designed to propel that stubborn little white ball toward a certain target several hundred yards down the fairway. If you think about it, there is not much to do, really. Swing the club, hit the ball, and watch the ball go!

On television every weekend, the pros can be seen performing this simple feat as if it were effortless. Yet most of us who play the game struggle and strain to keep the ball from landing in an area where it cannot be found again. As frustration takes over, we try harder. Muscles tighten. Blood pressure rises. Conversation becomes cryptic (I don't cuss, but where I spit, the grass doesn't grow). The old slice sets new records for distance—from left to right. Worms take cover, sand flies, water splashes, and sweat pours. How can a game that is so simple be so difficult?

Certainly many technical flaws may need to be worked out to correct a faulty game (G.A.S.—Grip, Alignment, Swing). But still, at the heart of it all, there are just a few simple principles to integrate in order for things to happen correctly. Above all, you need to relax, swing naturally and let your club do the work it was designed to do, understanding that all the mechanics must function in balance.

Throughout this book, we have looked at several important issues concerning the current state of pastors and churches. As in golf, the task of ministry can be somewhat simple or incredibly frustrating. Each of us must understand that real power for ministry, as well as living the Christian life, comes through Christ alone.

As a part of the Body of Christ known as the *church*, we must capture the moment at hand. For the Christian community, the 21st century will be a time of unprecedented challenge—and opportunity. While many of the changes that will occur could threaten the stability and capacity of the church to make an impact on our society, other changes are opening the doors for new forms of ministry.

Clearly, the Christian Body cannot hope to have

much of an impact if we respond in the same ways we have in the past. These are new challenges, demanding creative, unique responses. The solutions that worked ten or even five years ago will fail in the coming decade. We are being confronted with a new wave of obstacles and opportunities. After careful study of our options, and discerning the mind of God, we must tailor new strategies to address this new environment.

Have we reached the end times, graphically described in the book of Revelation? Jesus Himself told His disciples that no one would know when the final days would be; not even He knew when they would come. Futurists and self-proclaimed prophets who claim that they have identified the date of the final times are fooling themselves, if nobody else.

But our inability to foretell the exact timing of the end of civilization should not deter us from our appointed responsibilities. Every Christian has been gifted in special ways to perform specific tasks for the Kingdom of God. We are to work individually and corporately toward winning the world for Christ.

Nor should ignorance of the exact date of the coming judgment steal our passion for ministry and our sense of urgency about serving God. We ought to act as if these are the final moments of time, and make the most of the chances we have to share truth and salvation with others.

During this decade, the Church will be pressured from all sides to give up the battle. The intensity of the spiritual warfare unraveling in our midst will accelerate. Each of us will find it tougher and tougher to muster the courage, the excitement and the energy to combat evil.

An evaluation of the behavior of the American Church surely indicates that one reason we have had such a limited impact is that we have acted as a splintered Body, striving without vision and without a set of priorities for outreach. We cannot afford to make the same mistakes in the future.

While bringing this writing to a close, I'm sitting here at my computer with the television on in the background. The news event of the day is "Hurricane Katrina," which inflicted billions of dollars in damage to the Gulf Coast and caused untold misery and death.

No doubt there will continue to be hurricane-like forces that will threaten to dramatically alter the societal and cultural landscapes in which we live. These changes will be breathtaking, and some skeptics will even question if the Church and Christianity will survive.

Let there be no doubt—the Church of Jesus Christ

will not only survive, but will thrive! Jesus was and is the greatest change agent in the universe. The incarnation was and is the greatest union of revelation and relevance. John wrote, "The Word Became flesh and made His dwelling among us" (John 1:14). Jesus changes sinners into saints—the ultimate human transformation. He then forms those saints into the Church, "and the gates of Hades will not overcome it" (Matthew 6:18 NIV).

The Church of Jesus Christ could not be destroyed by Roman edict or Communist cruelty. It flourished under both. Christ's Church is extraordinary—changing with every generation, yet keeping the Gospel truth unchanged. No other institution comes close. Nothing compares to it, and all because Jesus Christ is God, the Church is supernatural, and the outcome is divinely determined.

You see, God views things much differently than we do. He sees a different battlefield and a different outcome than the one we see. He is in control! And, be sure of one thing: He reigns supreme over all elements of life, including the ministry of our churches.

We need to be happy and thrilled that He is willing to use us in His plan to reach fallen man.

As the twenty-first century begins, Christians are privileged to see God perform great acts through Christ's Church one more time—perhaps the best time of all!

Let us never forget the words of the beloved apostle Paul:

Take a good look, friends, at who you were when you got called into this life. I don't see many of the brightest and the best among you, not many influential, not many from high-society families. Isn't it obvious that God deliberately chose men and women that the culture overlooks and exploits and abuses, chose these nobodies to expose the hollow pretensions of the somebodies? That makes it quite clear that none of you can get by with blowing your own horn before God. Everything that we have—right thinking and right living, a clean slate and a fresh start—comes from God by way of Jesus Christ. That's why we have the saying, "If you're going to blow a horn, blow a trumpet for God."

You'll remember, friends, that when I first came to you to let you in on God's master stroke, I didn't try to impress you with polished speeches and the latest philosophy. I deliberately kept it plain and simple: first Jesus and who He is; then Jesus and what He did—Jesus crucified.

I was unsure of how to go about this, and

felt totally inadequate—I was scared to death, if you want the truth of it—and so nothing I said could have impressed you or anyone else. But the Message came through anyway. God's Spirit and God's power did it, which made it clear that your life of faith is a response to God's power, not to some fancy mental or emotional footwork by me or anyone else.

I don't want to hear any of you bragging about yourself or anyone else. Everything is already yours as a gift—Paul, Apollos, Peter, the world, life, death, the present, the future—all of it is yours, and you are privileged to be in union with Christ, who is in union with God (I Corinthians 1:26-2:5 and 3:21-23 MSG).

ENDNOTES

Chapter 1

[1]Hadden, cited by Ronald T. Allin, *Journal for the Scientific Study of Religion,* Vol. 9, N. 2, Summer, 1970.

[2]Former president of the Southern Baptist Convention Jimmy Allen, who has lost a daughter-in-law and a grandson to AIDS, and who has another grandson who is HIV-positive. Allen also has a gay son with AIDS. See "Judgmentalism Is Deadly to Human Relationships, *"Record: Newsletter of Evangelicals Concerned* (summer 1994); 1, as quoted in Martin E. Marty's Context (15 November 1994); 6.

[3]The inspiration for insight comes from Dennis Peacocke, who tells of jogging one day in 1997 and hearing the Holy Spirit judge his other-worldliness and fixation on the "end times" rather than the "ends of the earth": "'Dennis, you and I are going in opposite directions. I'm moving more and more to get *on* the Earth, and you're waiting to get off it.'" Dennis Peacocke, *Doing Business God's Way*: Almighty & Sons (Santa Rosa, Calif.: Rebuild, 1995), 5-6.

[4]Reggie McNeal, *The Present Future, Six Tough Questions for the Church,* Jossey Bass, 2003, pg. 82.

[5]Thom S. Rainer, www.churchcentral.com, *Ten Predictions for the Church by 2010*, Dec. 27, 2002.

[6]Selected statistics were taken from David Bryant, *The Hope at Hand: National and World Revival for the Twenty-First Century*, Baker, 1995.

[7]Used with Permission © 2000 - Shiloh Place Ministries, Inc. - All Rights Reserved PO Box 5, Conway, SC 29528-0005 Phone: 843-365-8990.

[8]George Barna, *The Second Coming of the Church*, Word, 1998.

[9] *Leadership Journal*, Spring Vol. 20, 1999, pp. 129, 130, Kevin A Miller.

Chapter 2

1 http://maranathalife.com/lifeline/stats.htm.

2 Erwin Raphael McManus, *An Unstoppable Force, Daring to Become the Church God Had in Mind*, Group, 2001, pg. 13-14.

3 McNeal, Reggie. *This Present Future*. Jossey-Boss, 2003.

4 Used with Permission © 2000 - Shiloh Place Ministries, Inc. - All Rights Reserved PO Box 5, Conway, SC 29528-0005 Phone: 843-365-8990.

Chapter 3

[1]Paul Dixon, *It is always Time to Forgive*, Cedarville Torch, "A magazine Ministry of Cedarville University, Fall, 1989, Vol11, No. 4, pg 2.

[2]The *Northwest Christian Times,* Pastoral Shortage and Increased Workload Places Burden On Clergy, September 2001.

[3]Ibid., pg. 2.

[4]Ibid., pg. 2.

[5]Doug Murren, *Churches that Heal, Becoming a Church That Mends Broken Hearts and Restores Shattered Lives,* Howard, 1999 pg. 18.

[6]Gary L. McIntosh & Samuel D. Rima, Sr., *Overcoming the Dark Side of Leadership,* Baker, 1997, 170-172.

Chapter 4

[1]The *Inland Northwest Christian News,* Enormous Loss of Pastors Reported, February 2003.

[2]Charles H. Chandler, *The Servant,* Volume 5, Issue 4, October 2000

[3]Rodney J. Crowell, *Musical Pulpits, Clergy and Laypersons Fact the Issue of Forced Exits,* Baker, 1992, pg.43.

[4]*Current Thoughts and Trends,* May 1999, pg. 14, NavPress, Colorado Springs, CO.

[5]Los Angeles Times, 01-29-99.

Chapter 6

[1]G. Lloyd Rediger, *Clergy Killers: Guidance for Pastors and congregations under Attack,* 1997, pg. 1.

[2]Henri J. M. Nouwen, *The Wounded Healer: Ministry*

in Contemporary Society, Doubleday, 1972, pg. 83-84.

Chapter 7

[1]Used with Permission © 2000 - Shiloh Place Ministries, Inc. - All Rights Reserved PO Box 5, Conway, SC 29528-0005 Phone: 843-365-8990.

[2]E. Glenn Wagner, *Escape from Church, Inc.,* Zondervan, 1999.

Chapter 8

[1]Carl F. George, *Prepare Your Church for the Future,* (Fleming H Revell Co. 1991) 13-15.

[2]Lyle E. Schaller, *Strategies for Change,* (Abingdon Press, 1993) 10-11.

[3]George Barna, *The Frog in the Kettle* (Regal Books, 1990) 29.

[4]George Barna, *User Friendly Churches* (Regal Books, 1991) 25.

[5]George Barna, *The Frog in the Kettle* (Regal Books, 1990) Back cover.

[6]Ibid., 26.

[7]Elmer Towns, *10 Of Today's Most Innovative Churches* (Regal Books, 1990) 12.

Chapter 9

[1]Reggie McNeal, *The Present Future, Six Tough Questions for the Church,* Jossey Bass, pg. 99-98.

Chapter 10

[1]Bill Hybels, *Courageous Leadership*, Zondervan, pg. 23.

[2]Erwin Raphael McManus, *An Unstoppable Force, Daring To Become the Church God Had in Mind*, Group, 2001, pg. 17-18.

[3]Erwin Raphael McManus, *Dare to Live a Life of Adventure, Seizing Your Divine Moment*, Nelson, 2002, pg, 46-47.

ENCOURAGEMENT DYNAMICS

The Ministry of Encouragement

Restoration: Helping pastors and their families recover from damaged lives and ministries.

Motivation: Offering help to churches and pastors in refocusing their energies for effective ministry.

Education: Giving sound biblical and relevant information for leadership and ministry development.

Encouragement Dynamics Ministers to Pastors by:

▶ Encouraging and supporting the discouraged pastor and his family.

▶ Connecting pastors to appropriate ministries to aid in their healing process.

▶ Educating and informing local church leaders and congregations about today's ministerial environment.

▶ Disseminating resources and cutting-edge ministry data and information to pastors and congregations.

Visit: www.encouragementdynamics.com

**To schedule a meeting
or to contact Gary Pinion write or email**

Encouragement Dynamics
2919 Troon Court
Richland, WA 99354
509-521-5014
gpinion@aol.com